The Way to Write Short Stories

The Way to Write Short Stories

MICHAEL BALDWIN

Elm Tree Books • London

ELM TREE BOOKS

Published by the Penguin Group
Penguin Books Ltd, 27 Wrights Lane, London W8 5TZ, England
Penguin Books USA Inc., 375 Hudson Street, New York, New York 10014, USA
Penguin Books Australia Ltd, Ringwood, Victoria, Australia
Penguin Books Canada Ltd, 10 Alcorn Avenue, Toronto, Ontario, Canada M4V 3B2
Penguin Books (NZ) Ltd, 182–190 Wairau Road, Auckland 10, New Zealand

Penguin Books Ltd, Registered Offices: Harmondsworth, Middlesex, England

First published in Great Britain by Elm Tree Books 1986
3 5 7 9 10 8 6 4

Copyright © Michael Baldwin, 1986

Printed in England by Clays Ltd, St Ives plc

A CIP catalogue record for this book is available from the British Library

ISBN 0—241—11766—6

for
DAVID POWNALL

Contents

Acknowledgments

The lines from *The Four Quartets* (p. 8) are taken from *Collected Poems 1909-1962* by T. S. Eliot, published by Faber & Faber Ltd.

Hump MacBride and Suicide and *The Gift* (p. 20-22) are taken from *My Organic Uncle* by David Pownall, also published by Faber & Faber Ltd.

How (p. 88) is © 1982 by M. L. Moore

The Bus of Dreams by Mary Morris (p. 89) is published by Hamish Hamilton Ltd.

Chapter One

Why and What Not

1. *In the Beginning*

Angus Wilson once said that he began his writing career with short stories because they were all he had time for. A novel seemed impossible to contemplate, but he could imagine completing a story during his weekends away from work.

Sid Chaplin did not want to write stories of any sort. He wanted to tell them. He was born among the mining villages of the North East where there is a strong oral tradition, and where the storyteller is one of the most highly respected members of the community, as influential as a clan bard.

Unfortunately, Sid Chaplin was a shy young man who fancied he had a speech impediment. He had — in the words of the old paradox — to take up his pen or hold his tongue.

None of us quite knows why we want to write, or not at the beginning. But once the determination takes hold of us, we have to do it. And of all the forms that suggest themselves, the short story appears the simplest and the most saleable.

For many people it proves to be neither, but it *is* short. Its problems confront us at once. They are not always easy to solve, but they can be identified. To abandon twenty chapters of a novel is a terrible experience. To make a hash of half a dozen short stories is to gain a very considerable

1

insight into many aspects of narrative form and style, as well as the ways in which we are going to operate in future.

2. *Sanity in brevity*

'Short story' is a reassuring term: it contains something of its own description and prescription, and although it asks to be treated with respect we can feel comfortable with it. If it is to be short, then we can ask how short. The mere fact of its shortness will, to a degree, determine what we mean by 'story': not a life study, not the total history of an endeavour, hardly a 'rich tapestry of scene, mood and character'. Brevity is a stern requirement, but it brings its own comfort. A *short* story may perhaps be so short that its success need not turn on its story at all. If it does, then surely that story can be a very simple one?

A simple story is as elementary as hopscotch. That is why Flaubert and Forster — tortuous minds both — hated it so much. Yet a basic linear story is what most usually gives movement to the short form, and it is the inability to provide this movement that often, quite unnecessarily, baffles newcomers.

Newcomers or not, I think we are quite ready to accept that 'story' and 'short story' are not necessarily the same animal, not even one animal inside the skin or belly of another. All fiction tries to tell 'a story'. Sometimes this story is simple and apparent; sometimes it is complex or buried deep in some spontaneous interplay of character. Yet, if we were asked to summarize either a short story or a novel, we should do so by explaining 'what happens'; in other words we should retell its 'story'.

There is a useful technical word to express this meaning of story, and it is already familiar to us even if we do not read literary criticism. It is 'plot'.

Some people put plot first. Others, both authors and critics, put it last. Others again — and I am one of them — prefer to think of it simply as 'part of the mix', a necessary but not always dominant ingredient.

Nonetheless, it is the one strand in fiction that is easy to recognize, even if we cannot always separate it; and it is particularly noticeable in a short story. Since we have to start somewhere, let us begin by trying to understand what plots consist of, and what makes them work.

The most usual, oldest and simplest plot is the linear. Some authorities call it 'the stair', 'the narrative arch', 'the boy across the wall'. I see nothing wrong with 'Linear Plot'.

3. *The simple linear plot*

A simple linear plot (and perhaps story) comes into being when the following requirements are met. A person or persons (or agreeable little dog) nurtures a wish, desire, need or objective. The fulfilment of this wish, desire or need, the gaining of this objective, meets an impediment. The impediment is overcome. The objective is gained or the wish is granted. End of linear plot (and perhaps story).

The linear plot has been likened to a rope which is presented to the reader rolled and ready for use; but once it is seized and unrolled there is a knot in it.

So, to continue the image, we want to cross a ravine. We fasten one end of the rope to a tree, tie a rock to the other end, then toss it towards the bushes on the opposite crag. The rope snags and the resulting tangle shortens it. The rock cannot reach the far side and dangles into the ravine (the impediment). We, or a passing troop of Guides, haul it up and disentangle it (the resolution): or we cadge a lift in a convenient helicopter (ditto) and eventually reach the other side. There may be a succession of impediments and resolutions; but given the single objective we are still riding the simple linear plot.

Its strength will come from the writer's ability to interest us in the central character and then to heighten that character's sense of purpose. The impediment itself need not be unexpected. If someone is trapped at the top of a burning building, for instance, it will not take much wit to place all manner of perfectly reasonable and expected impediments in the way of that person's survival. The skill

3

comes at the point of resolution, that is in finding a convincing way out.

Consider another chestnut. Many a person has been known to cool the heat of summer by taking a dip in an enticing reservoir, lake, tarn, stream, river or one of the seven oceans. It is not quite so predictable, outside the traditions of pub narrative, for that person to discover every stitch of discarded clothing stolen just before or just after the moment of chilly emergence from the pure serene.

Of course, it will be predictable (simple linear decoration) if we dwell on that person's coyness or timidity, youthful beauty, careful removal and folding of each elegant item of dress, and so on. If we stress the idea of nudity we encourage salaciousness. But nothing invalidates the story, if we can devise a clever and inevitable resolution of the predicament.

So, in the simple linear plot, the impediment can be expected or not, according to the strength of the original need. It is the resolution that needs to be unexpected. Or it must be if we are going to let the plot generate the main current in the story.

For the moment, it is worth noticing that in our three classic outlines the need, wish or objective quotient has been sharpened into a predicament. This is much more forceful than, say, a narrative line based on a random impulse to take the bus and visit Uncle Harry, even if it occasions the scorn of Messrs Flaubert and Forster.

Predicament implies both need and impediment: I must escape from this burning building; how can I leave the water without any clothes to put on? So it is quite possible to shorten the linear recipe to: predicament plus resolution.

4. *Scrambled or addled*

Our discussion so far has its own plot. It is this. Many people think that stories are difficult to make because they feel that plots are hard to find. In fact, plots are very easy to find, the simple linear being accessible to the point of triviality. So perhaps we shouldn't bother with a plot at all, since the story which merely tells a story belongs to a bygone oral tradition, whereas we inhabit a world which is post Joyce and Beckett, a world in which many writers, increasingly women writers, are trying to make literature from the hard facts of their lives. In the contemporary world, we could argue, the abyss is ever-present and the abyss can never be crossed; it is fatuous to look for a rope to sling over it because such a rope does not exist and the abyss probably does not have another side anyway.

Before we let ourselves become carried away with all this, it is worth noting that a number of significant processes were afoot in that paragraph. The linear's first major variant was given an airing: the pursued aim is either not attainable or, when attained, not worthwhile. Secondly, I used the phrase 'the story which merely tells a story'. That phrase may faithfully summarize the anti-plot position; but it is a palpable nonsense. Some writers do indeed wish 'to tell a story'. To tell a 'story which merely tells a story' is an impossibility.

This is because in all probability our plot will not perch itself on a clifftop. It will be in a kitchen, a bus, a launderette, a clinic, a school, a bank or a dole queue, somewhere in the recognizable streets or lanes. Its main character's needs will be the elimination of a commonplace dissatisfaction. The impediment will be another person, or the lack of some basic implement. The resolution may well be inconclusive and not very satisfactory. And yet that will make it a simple linear story just the same, although the plot will not exactly run on a turbocharger but get by on coffee, compromise and aspirin like the rest of us.

I said just now that to tell a story which merely tells a story is impossible. That is because it is unthinkable that our story should not be enmeshed in somebody's life. Once we do enmesh our story in a life, then the pressure on the plot becomes less. The impediment is bound to be real (we all meet a hundred of them a day) and its avoidance can be a long way short of the miraculous.

Take one of our artificial, strong plot situations — a person is about to be engulfed in a fire. The mechanics of the rescue are likely to swamp the story in improbabilities, to call for the intervention of a Superman or Wonderwoman,

5

unless our approach rests upon other values and different expectations. If the person is real then failure to escape is acceptable, though cruel. If he is a suicidal arsonist, then the threat may not be in the fire itself but in the quest for self-immolation. The latter can be set aside by a failure of will, a realization that he has made a hash of the insurance provision for his family, or simply forgotten to feed or strangle the budgie.

Such matters may still seem external, the properties of artifice — though if the brain is not made up of insurance and budgerigars, then what is it full of? The story we are writing will rest exactly on our answer to this and similar questions. How do we interpret our perceptions, our emotions, our day to day existence, life itself? Indeed, the moment our story starts to go wrong, it is worth asking ourselves just what we have done with our commonsense.

For the moment, we are looking to plot, the simple linear, to provide the first answer. If our commonsense refuses us a plot, but insists we explore our perceptions — of, say, worn-out blankets, the neighbour's electric drill, a blocked bathtub and a larder without sugar, all well and good — just so long as it keeps them worthy of our attention. But once the interest dulls, at the beginning of the very first paragraph which fails to transmute life into art, then we must ask what is the aim, what the impediment, and will there be a resolution? Even to proclaim that this story will be without them is to start the analysis somewhere. Indeed, it is one of the paradoxes of the form that although a short story begins with the very first word of its very first sentence, nothing need happen in it until the last, and what happens need be nothing.

This is a description of the linear's second major variant: the plot deferred. The writer must know it is there, the reader must be absolutely confident it is there, the Damoclean sword suspended above his head that may or may not drop.

Here in chapter one, however modern we are, we shall take a pinch of plot. We shall ask what our characters want and what is stopping them getting it. In drama it is called

6

conflict, and in a soap opera a little of it goes a long way; but just as with garlic or salt, life can be very flat without it.

5. *Flexing*

Some people read books in order to dream, even books like this. Some read in order to do. What kind of reader are you?

It may be that you intend to be one of the doers — intend to be, one day, tomorrow, perhaps. You will read this little homily, you will even read the authors I mention in the next chapter, and then — when you are quite ready to begin — you will take a long walk round the reservoir and think how, when and where and by what means this miracle shall come to pass.

Once, a long time ago, I used to teach as well as write. As a teacher I had what are known as 'colleagues' (a writer has no colleagues — axiom). One of these colleagues also wanted to write. They all do. He watched me looking broody. They all do. 'You're looking a bit down in the mouth,' he said.

I made a hideous mistake. I mentioned the story I was writing. 'I'm stuck,' I said.

'You don't know what happens next? What — in a story *you're* writing!'

As a matter of fact I don't always know. It sometimes takes me months to find out. But in this case I knew very clearly. I had my piece of string. I had arranged every knot in it to the last thieves' bend and collapsing sheepshank. 'It's not as simple as that,' I explained. 'What I have to do in the very next section is going to call in question the entire focus of the story, its style, its viewpoint, its . . . to be quite honest, it's making me reassess my whole theory of narrative.' I spoke at some length, with mounting fervour and accelerating pomposity.

He let me finish and then said quietly: 'As you know, I've got literary intentions myself. When I get down to putting them into practice, I'll make a point of being able to answer that sort of question before I let myself begin.'

I am afraid that that sort of question is posed by the piece of paper. If you want to have the answers before you confront yourself with the *real* question, *on paper*, you never will begin. Or, when you do begin, you'll find they are the wrong answers. The questions only pose themselves when you have begun. They are fresh questions, different answers. As Eliot says:

> . . . Every attempt
> Is a wholly new start, and a different kind of failure
> Because one has only learnt to get the better of words
> For the thing one no longer has to say . . .

All that any writer has is his experience. If you intend to write, start to get yourself some experience now.

Before you begin, you will please do yourself a favour. However poor you are, whether you type, write by hand on coloured cardboard or with a chisel on a wall, *resolve to use one side only*, and continue this as your life's habit.

You may not be able to afford much in the way of walls or paper, but you can't afford to have a brainstorm either. There is nothing worse than deciding that the end of something you have written is in fact its beginning, and that paragraph three will come better after you are shut in the bathroom cupboard, only to realize that you cannot transpose with scissor and paste and see what the new version looks like, because you've written on both sides of the paper. Even bricks can be rearranged, but not if you've written on both sides of them.

Perhaps you have been pondering away for some time, and only need to grit your teeth in order to get yourself going on plans that have already been laid.

If not, I suggest you consider one of the two following exercises. Unless you are very uncertain of yourself you will find them mutually exclusive; so it is worth selecting the one that is more attractive to you — it may point you towards your own maturing work processes.

Alternative One

Write a narrative account of a short part of your today. Write it in the first person (I did . . . I thought . . . I went . . . etc.) and begin at some point at which your clear wish or need meets with an obstacle. For example, you want to post a letter but haven't got a stamp; you are pushed to get to work and already late for the train; you need to make a decision but are short of vital information; you want to follow a certain line of action but your boss, your friend, or someone in the family thwarts you . . . something like that. Leave the narrative exactly where you think it should end, whether in satisfactory resolution or angry frustration. If you find this 'I' of yours taking on unexpected characteristics or becoming some other person, don't worry in the least. With or without this enrichment you will have manufactured a story around a simple linear plot.

Alternative Two

Write a description of a person you know. As soon as the description loses its bite, even if you have only written a sentence, assess the evidence you have placed on paper — or call on the information remaining in your head — to decide what this person could do, or have done to him or her, to keep the account interesting. In other words, you are going to take someone you know, set him in his own environment, and use him to generate a piece of action. *If* you feel like carrying the action through, you will have achieved a simple linear. If not, don't worry. It could be that you haven't a linear mind, or don't see the world in straight lines. Later chapters are going to discuss how characters can be moved through other than linear patterns.

Put your piece of writing away for a day or two, then take it out and simply tidy it up sentence by sentence. Make sure your words say what you want them to say, and that they are grammatical or stick to a consistent usage.

When they say what you want them to say, you may find that they still don't do what you want them to do. This is a common affliction. It can be cured.

If you feel entirely contented with your product, you have substantial grounds for alarm.

Chapter Two

Masterclass

1. *Outside in or inside out?*

It is usual to say there are two great traditions in the short story: one exemplified by de Maupassant (1850-1893) and one by Chekhov (1860-1904). The Frenchman gives us a strong linear plot with a sting in the tail — a poor woman borrows a rich friend's necklace, loses it, and puts herself and her husband in debt for life in order to raise enough ready money to replace it instantly without her friend knowing of its loss. Years later, when the debt has been repaid and she has been rendered unrecognizable by hard work and worry, the rich friend confides in her that the one she lent was only paste.

The Russian is less interested in plot, we are told, less ruthless and arbitrary with his endings, more given to exploring the interplay of characters in charged situations. A young student joins a party of friends on a brothel expedition. They do not like any of the girls in the first brothel, but spend some of their scant money supply on drink, dancing and music. They stagger from brothel to brothel, depleting their purses and growing drunker and drunker. When they at last discover the 'perfect brothel', the young student does not wish to join in the fun, and goes to bed not with a girl but with an awakened social conscience.

One author starts with plot, we are told, and one with

character. In reality, it is not as easy as that. That is why it will pay us to read through their collected works and ask ourselves which starts with which.

That time will not be wasted, whatever our conclusions. A writer needs to read. Unless we have the time and the energy to spend all day at our desk, we must learn to spend some of it in our armchair. Life may well be an author's oxygen, but reading is his blood. His veins must be full of literature. It follows, though, that we must confine ourselves to the books we can digest, and protect ourselves against the rest of them. We best know our own hemisphere, whether we need to read *with* or *against* our own current concerns, what will do us most good and influence us least. We need to be guided, not corrupted. People often give me books which they think will do me good — it's a natural act of friendship. I accept them gratefully and hide them on my shelf. I never read them unless they conform to my own diet sheet. This is not closed-mindedness; or, if it is, I am unrepentant. I may well come to them one day when I feel I have need of them. We must read what we need now.

What de Maupassant and Chekhov can teach us at once is that a good short story has space. Their best work looks deeply and roomily into lives and their circumstances, even in so brief a compass. They are prepared to let days, even years pass on a single page. A few years ago there was a new literalism afoot. It suggested that even a novel could not hold much. Event and reading speed should be closely related. Time must be held on a tight rein. If it was inconsiderate enough to want to gallop ahead then it should only be allowed to do so between chapters. Since a short story is a parsimonious fragment lacking chapters, it should be a slave of the clock. A man shaving and being irritated by a troublesome moth, a woman finding herself undecided about which shoes to slip on — these were seen as fitting subjects for the story. A quick sniff at de Maupassant puts paid to all that.

He is often held up as an example by contemporary purists. He may jump the fences and streams of place and time, but his plots move straight ahead, it is argued. We may agree with such a judgment but find it constricting. In which case, Chekhov offers an agreeable sense of *laissez-faire*.

For a start, his stories do, quite often, have chapters. That is, they divide themselves into distinct, sometimes numbered, sections. These gaps represents a shift of time, sometimes a change of viewpoint. Again there are purists who do not like these manifest holes in the narrative, these spaces on the printed page. All I can say is that literary art is much more to do with practice than theory, and the short story, of all forms, is the plaything of pragmatists. A glance along the shelf yields me Colette, Joseph Conrad, Milovan Djilas, Katherine Mansfield, Albert Camus, John Updike, Nadine Gordimer and Angus Wilson, all of whom have at various moments of need or inclination sectionalized their short stories.

Chekhov's most important shift is one of viewpoint. Often the core of his story is quite static. In *The Two Volodyas*, for example, matrimonial dissatisfaction is at the centre of things, and this does not change; but by its nature it demands the deployment of certain characters: the couple are essential, so is a 'third party'. Chekhov clearly does not think much will ever come of anything in this world, whether it is marital or extra-marital passion, or prayer; but by shifting the narrative viewpoint from husband, to wife, to husband, to wife and wife's lover, then back to husband and wife again, he gives a sense of movement, of life, to his deliberately lifeless theme. What his stories seem to say to us is, 'The world is a pretty dull place, but stick with me and I'll show you the drama of it.' In Chapter One I spoke of the sword of Damocles. Chekhov's technique, and his philosophy, exploit this to the full. His characters are frequently exclaiming that they are bored, not realizing that the cord is parting above their heads and the blade is about to fall.

He brings the commonsense of genius to his storymaking. This is what makes him so easy to learn from. Marriage may be dull. As a subject it may bumble from dump to dump. But a love affair is never static. So immediately, and by instinct, he translates boredom into adultery; and adultery for him is a moveable feast, constantly in progress, from bad, to very bad, to very much worse.

But I doubt if he starts here. He starts, I suggest, with a

sense of activity which is exterior to the plot and which will provide him with a plot even if nothing, in a linear sense, happens. His recipe would appear to be: take a group of people and place them in a fluid, preferably a mobile, situation: a quest, a gathering, a party, a journey, a sleigh ride. Then there is bound to be a sense of movement, even if nothing changes. But, in the nature of things, movement will bring change. It hangs its own sword above the reader's head.

Suddenly, our discarded idea in Chapter One does not appear at all bad: a girl goes on a bus ride to visit her uncle. She takes her best friend with her and she is in a story by Chekhov.

2. *Stereotypes and stereotyping*

Both de Maupassant and Chekhov are very near to us in time. If they had lived out even a modest three score years and ten we should think of them as belonging to our century; and yet they are presented to us as archetypes. Although literature and literacy in the West are well over two thousand years old, the short story is scarcely a hundred. It was born of stereotype presses and the demands of mass circulation publication; if ever a form was the child of its market and grew among working journalism this was it. Never mind *Susanna and the Elders* or *Cynewulf and Cyneheard*. They are not its ancestors: we are dealing with a new growth.

This should cheer us up. There are no thou shalts and no thou shalt nots, merely what we can make work. More than that, such an infant can muster modern godparents: twentieth century conventions, contemporary instincts, current technology.

So far the story can only come to us from the printed page or through the radio, but this need not limit what it pretends to be. It can be a single viewpoint or multi-viewpoint narrative (we are still indebted to Chekhov), be in the first, third or — most rarely — the second person. It may be a monologue or a dialogue, see itself as a document, a letter, a confession, a will, a court transcript, a print-out on a VDU;

it can present itself as a voice in the ear, voices overheard, or as something on a telephone, tape or answering machine; and the minute we relate it to its contemporary documentary possibilities, we begin to glimpse its advantages over the novel.

Most of these devices are not available to the novelist because they strain common sense the longer they continue. Quite a lot of Conrad's *Lord Jim* is meant to be oral narration. Fancy *listening* to those magnificent polysyllabics for 200,000 words, or exactly twenty hours. Yet in the Conrad short stories the heard, even the overheard, narrative is a perfectly acceptable pretence which the author exploits faultlessly on all manner of occasions. *The Brute* is a brief and accessible example of this, and it teaches us that the documentary — or what I prefer to call the evidential story (that is, the story which does not seek an immediate subliminal transfer between page and brain but makes use of a narrator or reprographic device) — really exists in three ever present layers: in other words it forces depth and dimension upon its author. There is the story that is actually told, the story within the story so to speak; there is the storyteller or the document, lending it character, value and style; and there is the circumstance of its telling, which generally includes a fictional audience.

Joseph Conrad (1857-1924) found it extremely hard to write. That is why he is so much help to us. English was his third, almost his fourth, language. In it, in his laboriously constructed sentences, he sought to resolve the conflict between ambition and ability. Most writers need to *imagine* themselves 'there' (very dull it will be for the reader if we don't): Conrad had actually to *be* there, as part of the audience in his riverside pub, as a minor witness in the story itself, more rarely a partially masked member of the narrative team. His 'there' was nearly always at some point of conflict between values. So his narrator acts as a sympathetic interpreter of the perceived aberrant (the story within the story or its protagonist) to the perceived norm (the circle of listeners who may or may not represent the reader's viewpoint).

This has been called multilateral fiction. Angel cake is a more memorable term; and it is only this ponderous analysis of its theory which makes it seem remote. If our story pretends to be a confession, we have to decide not only who is confessing and to what, but *to whom*. The audience inhabits the action, and if it is an oral confession the audience may take part in it and bring it to a linear full stop by cutting out the speaker's tongue or arranging a lynching party. The short story may be a sausage which has to fit its skin exactly, but the angel cake method lets us use more crumbs.

This may seem old-fashioned. Everyone can grasp and operate the sort of evidential story in which, say, a family gathers to listen to a will, but the will turns into a confession of lust and an accusation of greed. The matter is resolved (or carried forward) by an exasperated listener throwing the document into the fire. This is only another version of 'with one bound Jack was free' or 'Jill easily evaded his beastly clutches'.

True, but we are not speaking of ends, only of achieving a lot with a little. The main point to grasp about angel cake is the importance of the fictitious audience. The story may indeed be on a floppy disk, and we may gain words and tension from having our audience find it difficult to begin to unlock its message; there may be all kinds of play made with computer-speak and even computer malfunction, but we will need to know who that audience is. The layers of the cake belong to each other: they are not a random amalgam of dough.

Conrad's importance to us is that he stands at the beginning of this whole line of thinking. Character, plot and circumstance are as essential to him as to de Maupassant and Chekhov. But by the beginning of this century fiction was beginning to be as uncertain of itself as narrative poetry had become midway through the last. It had to say, 'I am manifestly here on this piece of paper; yet in what other sense can I claim to exist?' Transparent narrative was no longer the aim, because the cinema could transfer action straight to the brain without the intervention of words. So why were these words, what was this piece of paper?

Conrad's answer was the only one the technology of his time left open to him. 'These words are here because they are the record of a fascinating story told to me about an unusual person.' Like all new answers it is very old, at least as old as Chaucer. Surprisingly, I think we have escaped from that neurosis. Fiction is under so much pressure that it need only appeal to believers, and that leaves its practitioners free.

But we still have to invent stories and fill them out. Angel cake is fine plump food, and today, what with tape, disk and telephone we are hardly restricted to words overheard in a pub.

3. *The Third Tradition*

So even a brief consideration of our task has alerted us to three possibilities, each of them ample: there is the linear and its variants; the non-linear, a whole host of natural alternatives which we began to glimpse in our discussion of Chekhov, and which will be detailed over the next four chapters; and then there is the evidential or documentary story, the notion that the author needs to justify himself and his piece of paper to the reader. I traced this back to Conrad, simply because his short stories are constantly grappling with the problem; but in truth it is a dilemma as old as narrative fiction and certainly much older than the short story. Defoe and Richardson were obsessed with it.

It is fertile to us, because — as I said — our short stories can pretend to be transcripts of every kind of reprographic process available to twentieth century man. To become document-obsessed is to provide the angel cake with an almost infinite variety of fillings.

Ernest Hemingway (1899-1961) was not much given to angel cake — he discovered enough tension in his attempts to achieve transparent narrative in his densely mannered style — but *Death in the Afternoon* contains some embedded fiction: man-of-the-world Hemingway interpreting loathsome life to innocent us, by pretending to talk to an unworldly old lady; and that is an exact recipe. One of these stories

17

concerns a homosexual seduction. Man entreats young man to be his love. Young man resists for a time, but when he falls, he falls for ever.

The Italian author Alberto Arbasino (1930-   ) takes the same idea in his *Giorgio versus Luciano*, but he does not 'tell a story about them': he lets them tell their own story, lets it unfold in a sequence of short paragraph lengths from each man, sometimes of externalized statement, sometimes of interior monologue.

This is not a play. Nor, in any previous sense, is it a short story. It does not pretend to be linear narrative nor a document. It does not attempt to justify itself for being something else. It assumes that it has something interesting to say and that this is the best way to say it.

Alex Hamilton (1931-   ) gives us the same sort of thing in his extremely powerful *Beam of Malice*. A soldier and his officer discuss the operation of their searchlight. Everything is in dialogue, its language terse, characteristic and eventful. It could be a play, but it is a play best suited to the armchair. Nothing happens onstage or *in* the dialogue. The dialogue narrates events. The event is murder by means of the searchlight beam.

My own *Sebastian and other voices* is another attempt to improve on angel cake. Frequently, as in *Confidential* or *A Review*, I achieve no more than a fresh serving of the original recipe. The first is a series of letters, reports and statements of account between a husband and the private detective who has been instructed to watch his wife; the second is a Sunday newspaper review of the Autobiography of God, to the interlinear merriment and exasperation of the literary editor and religious affairs correspondent. In *Entries*, though, I am with Arbasino and Hamilton: a pair of Siamese twins soliloquize about what is to become of their body corporate and their wife when the sick twin dies. This story is without narrative framework. It is a fugue for voices.

It strikes me, though, that there is many a possible variant for the old-fashioned documentary story. Angel cake is far from going stale. In real life, plots often become entangled in each other. A *real* angel cake has more than three layers.

18

How frequently must doctor's surgeries be invaded by people who claim to be seeking a cure for bad backs but who actually wish to discuss their emotions or their pockets? The beggar does not always want money, but sympathy. His begging ploy is often a detailed code of his inadequacies, an exact template of his pride. In *Special Relationships*, I have a vicar tell us where he stands on Christian Unity, the miracles, the place of the church in society, and the relationship of his local church council to the church. But he is really considering where his adulterous love for Miss Elsie Price fits in with his reverential scheme of things.

So, if we use a fictitious narrator, there is another question to be asked. Not *who* is he that he should be telling us this, but *why*, what is his real motive?

As we make our rough jottings for any documentary situation we should pencil in: what is it? What does it tell us? Who wrote it (dictated it, programmed it, or whatever)? Why ostensibly? Why in fact?

Those questions, born of our reading, will often take us straight into our story. For example, we imagine a girl writing a letter to her mother, and then subject both of them to a cross-examination in those five points and consider how the answers will affect the tone and style of the letter, what clues there will be within it, and whether the letter is the story, or whether it should be answered.

Mere paperwork, some people will object. There is a world outside the window. I am afraid paper is where writing happens. The walk round the block is an excuse.

4. *The Linear yet lives*

As I said earlier, the areas of doubt have contracted. It is no longer necessary to proselytize, simply believe. Alex Hamilton is not marooned in experiment. He also writes linear, atmospheric stories, and as such he should be read, especially by anyone who is impatient with philosophy. Hamilton has had his self-debate, no doubt; but he never lets it contort his narrative. He is worth seeking out as a stylish exemplar of what can be done.

Hemingway, too, is a fine traditionalist. For those who find him sexist, there is *Hills like White Elephants*, the sparseness of its enterprise being such that it conveniently fits any theory of the short story you care to apply to it.

David Pownall (1938-   ) is the best writer of the contemporary linear I can think of. *My Organic Uncle* (Faber, 1976) is a collection to treasure. It contains two perfect examples, in *Hump Macbride and Suicide* and *The Gift*, of the foiled linear and the linear with the sting in its tail. Guy de Maupassant would enjoy the latter.

Hump Macbride's job in a Zambian copper mine comes to an end, and as a result his family leave him. He resolves to commit suicide, but in a magisterial, eloquent fashion. He proposes to use his severance pay to finance a drinking spree which will usher his liver with the rest of him attached into its coffin. Belt, his African servant, is put on notice but given enough interim money to arrange for his employer's drunken retrieval from the bars and hotels each night — Belt collects him in a wheelbarrow — and for his ultimate burial.

Hump becomes famous. He is the champion drinker in an environment of champion drinkers. People come from miles away to challenge him to drinking competitions or to witness the carnage. Huge wagers are laid. Bar takings soar. Each night Belt gathers him unconscious home.

Unfortunately Hump's liver outlasts his purse. He is a failure even in his quest for death. Sorrowfully, he sets about sacking Belt. Belt refuses to leave him. What with the wagers, the tips, and a little deferential passing of the hat around each wondering assembly before collecting the unconscious gladiator in his wheelbarrow, Belt is now a very rich man.

> Inside the bag was money, notes, coins, even cheques. From even a cursory glance Hump could see that it was a small fortune.
> 'You saved that for me?'
> 'Of course. Fifty-fifty. We're partners.'
> Hump sat down on the side of the bed, his head in his hands. For a long time he stayed that way, looking between

his feet. Far away, in the dim country of his memories, he heard the laughter of the two children and remembered what it felt like to want to die. But when Belt squatted down before him and forced the raising of his head, the African saw that the man was smiling.

This is the end of the story. You will notice that the narrative does not hang about, but bangs on with what it is after. There are many things to savour in this story, beginning with its first lines:

He made up his mind to die.
Petal, his wife, and her two little girls, had upped and left him. . . . .

A reader finds it hard to relinquish a story that grabs so quickly at his sympathies.

The Gift is longer, but simpler to summarize. A British Agricultural Officer makes a present of an English stud bull to an African chief so that he may enhance the bloodstock of his mangy cattle. Arranging the transfer of this muscular piece of breeding mechanism from Hereford to Zambia proves to be a daunting task, and supervising its journey up-country is even more difficult.

Officer and bull reach the tribal lands to find a vast crowd assembled, and six cows waiting in crude mating pens. In spite of his fatiguing journey, it is absolutely essential, for political reasons, that the bull should begin at once, the chief explains.

The Agricultural Officer demurs. He, if not the bull, has a headache; but the chief insists.

The Officer gives way. To his surprised delight, Stoke Bliss Lad does not let England down. With a great moo of triumph he leaps on to the first cow, only to break her back. This sorry confirmation of the unsuitability of beast to beast is repeated five times. The Agricultural Officer retires his headache to a specially prepared hut.

When he emerges, refreshed from sleep, and ready to offer the herdsmen some considered advice, he finds that

21

the chief and his elders have already reached a political solution. Stoke Bliss Lad is being cooked as the centrepiece in a tribal feast of celebration and thanksgiving for the gift from across the waters.

5. *More travail*

David Pownall would probably not approve of that summary. For a start it falsifies his point of departure. The actual story begins like this:

> Anderson looked at the cow.
> Even though he was a professional, an acknowledged expert in stock-breeding and the science of animal husbandry, he managed to be fond of cows as cows. Unlike most farmers and agriculturalists he refused to call cows 'beasts'. In his heart he loved them for their peaceable, slow natures, their sweet odours, their great still eyes. Nothing was further from the concept of beastliness. They were steady, wholesome paradigms of good behaviour.
> But this one was an exception.
> It was the most unlovable cow he had ever seen.

Obviously, I needed to condense in order to compress twenty pages into a couple of paragraphs. Once the action begins I am true enough to it. Well, in general I am. There are some sequences that my version takes no account of. Then, alas, we have to consider my travesty of his ending. The facts are the same. They would not get me into trouble in a court of law: it is just that Pownall avails himself of a Chekhovian shift of focus to present them differently. He leaves Anderson asleep in his hut, and gives us this as a final paragraph:

> Mtebanika painlessly destroyed the massive bull with one shot from his father's old elephant gun and soon afterwards the air was sweet with the smell of prime British beef roasting over an open fire.

My version, abbreviated though it is, makes some assumption of circumstance and motive which can at most only be *inferred* from the original. I have taken Pownall's story and told it differently, just as doubtless he could have done himself had he been so minded.

So my first suggestion for activity in this chapter is that you should take hold of someone else's short story and retell it. Any old nineteenth century stock must be ripe for updating; or why not seize upon someone with a strong stylistic presence such as Nadine Gordimer, Katherine Mansfield or Angela Carter, read one of their stories once, then *rework* it — not merely summarize it — in your own fashion?

If your own work is already on the boil, then why not try to do something in two different ways, say from the viewpoint of another character (this will not be wasted, because Jack's story is never the same as Jill's, so you will in fact be extending your *oeuvre*)?

But in our beginnings, when plots are hard to find, it is quite in order to borrow one. We are not going to steal by publishing, unless we have so disguised the theft that it becomes a creation in its own right. When Chandler wanted to earn money as a short-story writer, he recast some work he found in *The Black Mask* magazine until he understood what he was about. When he wanted to learn to write thrillers he rewrote two novels by his friend Erle Stanley Gardner. He is a much better novelist than Gardner; probably because he took more trouble to understand Gardner than Gardner took to understand himself.

My second suggestion is to do with angel cake. Turn back to the five questions I said we should ask of a girl writing a letter and of the mother receiving it (p. 19). It does not have to be a mother and daughter, and, of course, it need not be a letter either. What is done need not be sent, nor if sent received. There should be plenty here to tease out on a piece of paper.

One more word. I am going to be arbitrary, but professional writing is. Pick a market length and write exactly to it. The most useful length is 2,250 words, the span of the

BBC broadcast story, though it fits other markets as well.

Whether the story is borrowed, written to the above prescription, or is the one you've been bursting to write, you will know that within just a few pages you must introduce your characters and put them in a situation and move the interest ahead.

Chapter Three

Finding a Story

1. *Words on the page*

One word on the page is worth a whole story planned in the head. I am not saying we should not plan, especially if we can think in sentences, paragraphs, snatches of dialogue. But if we do think in words, then it is necessary to snare them on paper as quickly as possible. Wordsworth could compose a poem while out walking, but a poem is its own memory system. That wonderful free-flowing story kicked out to the rhythm of a heart-beat while we were striding over the Pike has a nasty habit of sticking in the pen and congealing there altogether once we are back home. We clear mind and desk for action and it is suddenly as insubstantial as an after-dinner speech delivered in a dream.

So of course keep a notebook and carry it everywhere. It is our first commitment to authorship. For a long time it will contain nothing; but if we get used to opening it, then one day we shall find it has filled itself up. Write down snatches of conversation overheard on the train; try to devise an exact notation for the local dialect; describe rags, riches, beautiful and unbeautiful people down to the last unfastened button; and don't miss the lop-tailed cat, the coatless dog. If the notebook remains empty, write an exact inventory of the interior of the neighbourhood supermarket, the nearest church and a really loathsome back alley; and learn from nose, mouth and skin as well as from the more genteel eyes and ears. A church, a supermarket and an alley not only smell different, they feel distinct underfoot or beneath our heroine's forced down face. The more we enquire at large the more we are likely to blunder on a story. Record the taste of a church? How about *The Man who eats Prayer Books* for a title?

The notebook will begin to take longer each day. This is because to keep any sort of inventory, whether notebook, diary or scrapbook, is bit by bit to transform our whole way of looking.

I believe in cultivating the notebook, because it can become a powerful dynamo for people who believe they have nothing to say. People who have masses to say need not keep a notebook, but they should still learn to write everything down, or they'll soon have less.

Nowadays I make a point of never being too far from my desk; but anyone finding themselves swimming naked a mile off-shore when the words come should scratch them immediately on a companion's back or bite them into the dorsal fin of a great white shark. Nothing ever lasts in the head.

2. *Stories galore*

For the moment the notebook is no more than a bruise against the hip. We are going to open our writing pads and find where the stories are. Not the plots, not necessarily the beginnings, but the fragments which will become inspiration. We are going to find them in words and set those words down. The next three chapters will teach us how to order and expand those words.

So this section will contain a list of suggestions.

For each suggestion I shall give an example. You will make up and record your own examples.

Short stories often depend upon the character of a single person. The story grows from the character. If we can remember or invent and record a person, then we can begin to glimpse the story.

26

Here are some examples from my notebook. In the first one, I have not bothered to consider the language, merely the idea:

She was fifty but well preserved, well made-up at least. He was about sixteen. His body quivered as if he suffered from a nervous disorder and his face was fixed in a lopsided grin. He rested his mouth on her shoulder and it dribbled. 'He's the most considerate lover I've ever had,' she confided, 'and of course his father is so brilliant at chess.' She always managed to attract the most incredible people and say such surprising things about them.

This is from thirty years ago, so I do not feel shy of secrets. I knew her, so 'she *was* fifty'. I did not know him, so he 'was about sixteen'. Since this is a manifest character-sketch I keep it all of a paragraph, rather than break paragraphs between the two of them as I would if it were part of the narrative.

The story is somewhere in that fragment. It could speak of an eccentric woman, of a person who collects strangers or bizarre sexual partners. Or it could quite simply narrate the impediments (linear or foiled linear) of a difficult relationship fulfilled or otherwise. Or perhaps there is some concealed angel cake present. A cynical narrator (myself) is wilfully misinterpreting the healing love of a saintly woman for a malformed boy. Or perhaps she keeps the son in order to buy the father: she secretly plans to become a Grand Master at chess.

My notebook character was seen in some detail (and this confirms the value of keeping a notebook); but a superficial, even arbitrary description of a person can throw us into a story just as well:

It wasn't really a lisp; but he had a damaged front tooth and was shy about it, so people thought he was shifty.

Some writers will dislike this, not solely bcause it is shallow but because it changes its focus from the character's view of

27

himself to other people's opinion of him. This is too much for a single sentence, some will argue, too much even for the space of a story, others will say. Let us pretend that it is a choric sentence right at the beginning of the narrative. It is the equivalent of the establishing shot at the start of a film. If it is this, then I for one can work with it. My nameless person will make the world come to love him, either by seeking the help of his dentist or by growing a moustache. Or perhaps his slippery looks will cause him to be falsely arrested for the crime of the century, then paid an enormous sum in compensation (shallow beginnings leading to shallower ends).

I have wasted quite a deal of writing time objecting to sentences like the above, and much of my work is born of that objection. Let us not argue about it, save to say this: if we believe that a story should be single viewpoint and peep from inside a solitary skull or over one person's shoulder, then we are confining ourselves to the linear.

Let us not be so restrictive.

The simplest non-linear progression — let me call it the duplex — is to bounce the story back and forth between two characters. They can be just as trivially seen:

Mark was a day short of his forty-third birthday when the doctor made him put spectacles on.

He immediately began to hunger at life through shrunken, stone-bright, sexually attractive, newfound eyeballs.

Mary already wore glasses. In the morning they made her face shine as if it had been scrubbed all over with toothpaste. As the day wore on she seemed to haze away and freeze behind them into an icy lump of intelligence. Words fell awful and dangerous from her tongue like floes from a glacier.

This has become a game on paper, a paperchase; but I know where it will take me. I am writing *a story*, so it transmits its observation into action. Mark is not a man who wears spectacles. He is *made* to *put* them on. He *hungers*. Mary is seen from the outside (or so far she is), presumably by Mark rather than the narrator, because narrators see all things equally. But Mary is also a doer. She makes moods happen (or her glasses do), and hostility falls from her mouth.

Incidentally, this fragment began differently. It came to me in my car, my dictaphone was out of batteries, so I had to wait for home. It is now too wordy. I saw it as being less elaborate:

> When Mark put glasses on he became sexually attractive for the first time in his life.
> Mary already wore them and they made her seem aloof.

This is too terse. More significantly, it has a different emphasis that sets up other expectations.

What I have said so far is that a simple idea about a character can be played with on the page until it begins to turn into a story. We can do exactly the same thing with place. Let us mix some smell into this description:

> The stubble had been burned and turned under the plough, so Four Acre should have been breathing its autumn odours: carbon and flint and lime-leavened clay.

That one word 'should' sets up expectation, and it is the story-teller's delight to disappoint expectation, so I suggest that Four Acre should go on to stink like a buried herd of bullocks, or leak a strange miasma from the gums of its rotting furrows.

Two questions bring on the story: *why?* and *who first notices the stink?*

> Grindle Scar was the boldest cliff in the Pennines. There was fine free climbing to its Eastern lip, and some mechanical wizard had festooned the Great West Slab and Overhang with ironmongery before putting up an artificial 'first' that resembled Humber Suspension Bridge dangling from one end. No-one had found a route up the centre.

'Fine,' I hear you say. 'But aren't we already in the next chapter? Aren't we writing the beginnings of stories rather than finding them?'

In the case of Mark and Mary, perhaps. In the other examples I am less certain. When I know who is going to encounter the odorous field, or be tiger enough to power up the Central Buttress, I'll know where to begin. I may introduce the character to the reader first. It is not an inexorable rule that a sentence that carries the brain into the story should be the one where the story starts, or even have a place in the completed story at all.

3. *The Bloody Great Wheel and the Barrage Balloon*

When I was a child, our village became full of barrage balloons. They would rise on moaning cables high into the sky or sink down and be tethered in uneasy sleep at each lane's end. The major recreation of all the local children was to hinder the RAF regiment in their smooth operation. We would flock underfoot while they moored them, inflated them or flew them. When the airmen broke for tea we helped ourselves to their military rock cakes. Several older sisters helped themselves to airmen as well.

On windy days the balloons were hard to manage. They could be winched close to the ground, but then they would gyrate and roll like prehistoric beasts, and it needed a classroom full of children and a couple of stout teachers to swing on their handling ropes and peg them to the ground.

Once several of us were jerked off the ground high into the air. Fortunately we all kept our heads and hung on. Fortunately, too, the balloon did not break away.

I wrote a number of stories around those balloons, and used them in a novel.

A couple of years later I was standing with Maurice Bence, my history master, when a balloon broke away from an escort vessel in the river and began its long journey to the stratosphere and final exhausted explosion. This was always happening as balloons were transferred from boat to boat, or from ship to shore. On this occasion the balloon took a ship's boy aloft. He was reassembled a few days later in East Thurrock.

Maurice used to write radio stories. His pen-name was David Bruce. 'That is one of the two perfect plots,' he observed. The subject seemed rather raw, so I asked him what the other one was. He thought a bit, then said he had always called it 'the Bloody Great Wheel'.

He explained that if a writer took some characters and placed them in a fairground wheel he would always have a story. Better still if it was one of those rotating lift cages of the sort that rises so menacingly aloft in *The Third Man*. Or an ordinary lift would do, or a walk up the Eiffel Tower.

'That's not many stories,' I objected. 'The reader will very quickly grow tired of the Eiffel Tower.'

'It's a symbol, you dolt, like de Maupassant's coach-journey or Chekhov's ride on a sleigh. You put your characters in a situation like that and something will always seem to happen, even if nothing does.'

I drew him out and found he was full of all sorts of situations: a rock-climb, a caving expedition, children tripping across a flooded chalk pit on a raft, an elephant ride, two people inside a camel skin, even a ride round the Inner Circle. The moving event could represent a solo predicament — a linear; or the focus could bounce from person to person, from hind legs to head — a duplex.

The balloon was just a tiny smudge in the sky so I felt I could return to it. 'What did you mean by that?' I asked.

'Just an image of another sort of story, a refinement on the Bloody Great Wheel. The Barrage Balloon is not merely a symbol of encapsulated movement but of movement to disaster.'

'Like the bar of the sinking *Titanic*?'

'Exactly. Put it like this: one sort of story is about people trapped in a lift. The other is about a lift that comes off its hook.'

'All very arbitrary, surely?'

'It depends what you do with it. But in my experience that sort of story can never go entirely wrong. And for the writer it is almost as good as being hanged in the morning: it concentrates the mind wonderfully.'

It is worth collecting examples of both sorts of plot in our notebooks. They may never be needed. But those who cannot make a story move or gather life should remember Maurice Bence's view that 'that sort of story can never go entirely wrong'.

4. *Strong event*

Every so often we have the feeling that we have just witnessed something quite out of the ordinary. Often it is very ordinary indeed, but somehow it pricks our sensibility. We must learn to exploit it. We are bound to find our best inspiration in heightened moments. We will write most sharply about what we most clearly perceive.

A trivial example. I was once in the dentist's chair in an agony of apprehension. The receptionist/dental nurse was beautiful: that was why she was there. She was also clumsy and flustered: that was not why she was there. Suddenly I became aware that there was a sexual tension between her and the dentist and back again. It was quite as resonant as the rasp of the drill. I was appalled to realize that they were lost in each other and acting out an intricate ritual of self-awareness above the enormous crater he was digging in my head.

There is a story there. It involves all three people, and the summary gives us most of it. It also gives us one word too much: sexual. The nature of the tension needs to unfold itself slowly to the victim in the chair, the involved spectator. Perhaps it will never be entirely clear.

This is not necessarily angel cake. The person in the chair is in too intriguing a situation for him (or her) to be the narrator. Indeed, to make this a first person affair is only a first thought. Second thoughts are likely to be best.

It is possible to argue that first person accounts rarely do amount to angel cake anyway. There needs to be a fictional audience as well as a narrator.

I was in a small supermarket in South West London. There were three, perhaps four women assistants and a male manager. He was, on past observation, a tickler of ribs, a pincher of bottoms. He was not a gentle character with absent-minded hands like the waiter in the famous O. Henry short story. He was much too self-aware.

The girls were holding a protest meeting about him down at the till-point on this occasion. A story was pending, so to speak, so naturally I hovered.

His target was a small girl with dark hair. She was hot faced, and something had clearly been going on. The other women were trying to slow him down. He told the girl to bring the account book up to his flat above the shop. She refused, and the others reinforced her. He shrugged and told her instead to put some tins up on a top shelf. This necessitated her climbing a ladder; and I assumed it was a simple power play on his part, and that he was saying in effect, 'I mayn't be able to get you to come upstairs, but I'm certainly going to show you who's boss here.' It was all in character.

At that moment or just after (as Conrad would say), there came the clear sound of flesh being smacked or punched followed by the clatter of falling cans. I turned round and the girl was already being held clear of the floor and cradled unconscious in his arms. She was bleeding from a cut face. I suggested an ambulance. He brushed me and the women aside and carried her straight upstairs.

I think there is angel cake there. If I were to set the story out over three thousand words for you alone (and not invite an enraged Zoe Fairbairns or Michele Roberts to constitute the third slice), I should have continually to readjust my interpretation of the actors and myself as witness. It is obvious to cast the manager as a sexist villain. Perhaps the truth is more complex than that.

Notebook situations are rarely so full. I went to a health shop in Chiswick to buy some garlic capsules for my mother (you see how many strands are already entangled? Anything can take a plot away: this is why, finally, every word in every sentence must be considered). I was young then. The manager looked pretty ancient, say forty. He sold me the capsules, then served a woman with oil of evening primrose and told her this was the elixir that kept him so young and

33

beamish. She evidently thought as I did, so asked him his age. He said he had buried three wives and was ninety-seven. The woman did not believe him. But titles are so important. I would call this one *Sales Talk*.

A cat is trying to halt the turntable of my record player, and across the road a piano is playing in an unfurnished, derelict house. A woman has just been thrown from her overturned car and her family are bleeding, yet she is searching for the contents of her spilled handbag. A party of soldiers pacing to the rifle range beyond the dunes at St Ives overmarches two nudes in a hollow of sand. A drunken poet arranges to meet a girl by a tree, and she waits for him all night in the rain while he lies unconscious in a nearby ditch. The soup bubbles in the huge tureen and from inside it a manual alarm clock rings; and another alarm sounds from a box of geraniums above a college quadrangle while young men and women in evening dress sing *Arise ye subterranean winds, arise*. Three of us — myself and two women who impersonate young children (one is in *The Archers*) — sit cutting a record for the British Council downstairs in the BBC: there is a countdown while the wax rotates, then one by one we are overtaken by a fit of the burps. An old man dies on a snowy pavement in Stratford East. No-one stops to help him except a black girl who speaks no English. The phones are out of order. I finally get a taxi to take him to casualty for ten pounds in advance. I lecture English teachers in Dusseldorf high under a wooden roof on the hottest day of summer. A girl's face haunts me. I come back to England and meet two men who have left Germany because of her. I take a badly beaten, concussed woman to casualty at the Royal Free, and everyone assumes that I am the man who has injured her. When it is established that I am the one who rolled her from under the stamping boot, it is then assumed that I am her lover and that it is on my account that an imagined husband savaged her. When they have finished dressing her wounds, she asks to see me. She holds my hand and a young nurse stands crying at the door (question: what story did the woman really tell?). I exit left from the first shoot of Lord's Rake but somehow miss the West Wall

Traverse. Clinging to Scafell Buttress with only God beneath my boot I meet someone I have not seen since childhood . . .

These are fragments from a life's notebooks. Everyone has similar memories. What I know about all of them is that they are short stories, something I can consider and tell in a few thousand words. There are linears there, and a duplex, together with at least one angel cake. The 'I' is there frequently, because they are incidents that have happened to me or that I have known happen. In most cases the 'I' will disappear or become a fictional one.

If you ponder some of these pieces of my life, you will see that they are not necessarily beginnings, and even more rarely ends. Nonetheless they can be teased into shape with a little thought and much hard work.

5. *So I told her straight . . .*

There are very few writing games to help the author of short stories. I used to set myself an exercise I cribbed from L. A. G. Strong; and I shall offer it in a moment. But writing games are best played in company, and fiction is a lonely craft whose best aid is boredom. If we join writing circles we do so to read and discuss, not to play games.

There is a great deal of beginner's benefit to be had from writing a page of narrative on a set subject, say 'An Argument with a Bus Conductor' or 'Fishing in the Rain'. What happens then is that we talk through in *detail* what we have done, to the writing circle, a friend, or to ourselves. (I think it was Malcolm Lowry who said, 'I can't get to work here: I can't think aloud.') Other people's opinions are of scant importance to us — it is only an exercise, after all. What is important is to *understand* what we have done, *to the last comma*. Why is it all in short sentences? Why haven't I given the woman a name, and why — having established that her daughter is called 'Sarah with an aitch' — do I subsequently always call her 'she'?

I thought we were finding a story. We are. There is always a story to be found in writing exactly, because it involves understanding exactly. At some moment we become interested in this woman we have invented, the mother who insists her daughter is 'Sarah with an aitch'; and at that point fiction will take hold of us and not leave go until we have done our duty by it.

What we are overhearing the woman do is *speak*. There are all kinds of stories in overheard speech, even if the words are only overheard in our head. It is excellent practice to write dialogue and read it aloud. The most interesting tyro's talk is an argument; better than that a blazing row. It will provide us with first class material and prevent us from wasting too much money on psychotherapy if we complete on paper every little verbal explosion the day blesses us with.

L. A. G. Strong's little ploy? Yes, when the stories failed to come he used to set himself to write about any three objects, chosen at random but sequenced to make a plot. It is a device that tired schoolteachers have long since adopted without caring about the source.

Without caring about the exact procedure as well. Strong only cites one instance of this really working for him: he was on a seaside holiday and bored enough to write anyway. His 'objects' weren't really the classteacher's sword, skull and Spanish fan, either, but much more the sort of *incident* or *circumstance* that you and I might jot in our notebook.

His hotel was on a headland, at one side of which was a beach of red stones. On the other side the beach was white. There was a young cricketer staying at the hotel, and this young man had a phenomenally accurate throwing arm. There was also a man with a dog that had been trained to retrieve golf balls.

In Strong's story, a man falls over the cliff on to the red beach. Strong's detective deduces he has been murdered (his villain an amalgamation of cricketer and dog trainer) because a white stone lies near the corpse on the red pebbles.

To achieve the same result, we should place together two or three jottings *from our notebooks*. The harmonizing factor will be our own unique viewpoint. When we make a note our mental computer is already beginning its programme, so our notebook is where we should turn for Strong's 'fragments of inspiration' if we want to play his game. We shall soon find it is no longer a game.

6. *'It was not raining . . .'*

Novelists often begin with the rain. Stories abound concerning rainfall and so-called 'writers' block' (in my case another term for indolence). A certain famous novel — ah! but which one? — would never have been started if water had not dribbled on the window-pane, and there are authors who claim they can only begin a new project when the storm clouds gather and the high midsummer pomps begin to rinse down the gutters. 'It was raining' is the archetypal first sentence, or so I used to be assured by academics who were expert in the operation of the Muse.

This has led me to inscribe the following sentence whenever I cannot begin:

'It was *not* raining.'

I then go on with a little gentle parody of whatever author I hold responsible for my state of mind. Hemingway, for instance:

It was not raining.
I was on the way to see Rob.
Rob used to be my friend but she wasn't now.

Then, to keep my template in place, I use it to trace out the kind of narrative that its rightful owner would never in any circumstance indulge in:

Rob used to be my friend but she wasn't now.
(Rob as in old-fashioned Roberta.)
Rob was getting married.
She was getting married to my last husband but one.
Or she was unless I could be there to stop her.

My imagination is now caught by a word forced upon me by the need to avoid too much repetition — even in a parody of Hemingway. Why did I write such a metaphysic word as 'be'?

Unless I could *be* there to stop her.

Am I trapped in a ghost story? a dying coma? a drugged haze? I can now tear the exercise into tiny pieces and begin.

This brings me to a stratagem every bit as rewarding as the ones which have concluded previous chapters. It is a kind of prose *bouts rimés* or pass-the-parcel, only the writer plays it alone.

A sentence must be found and its meaning extended *intelligently* and *dramatically* until a story suggests itself:

It was not raining.
Robert kept a Gardeners' Diary. He had begun it with the year, and the year began with rain. There seemed little point in mentioning rainfall then, in January, say, or February, when the flowerbeds swam with wet and the bulbs were shod in rot.

So far it is atmospheric but hardly eventful. Robert must do something. He must be levered out of the past historic.

Robert thumbed page after page, wondering at what point his failure to mention rain disguised the fact that no rain fell. Was it as early as March that his drought had begun?

The diary is a prop, so it has to be used. 'Page after page' is a cliché that already offends. I wanted to add: 'Had it really started in the wet'; but paused because of the repetition. I could change one of my 'wets' to 'mud', but this will still leave Robert afflicted by a stilted turn of mind. *If* I decide that is right for him, that this story should concern itself with mania among the droughty geranium boxes, I'll include it after all.

This is only an exercise, yet it helps to make us aware,

stage by stage, of the way a short story builds itself up on the page; and the fact that its style must retain its fragile, nervous relationship, statement by statement, with the reader.

By extending a trivial proposition and attempting to convert it to narrative we learn to become the reader over our own shoulder. If we find ourselves blind to our own foibles or cluttered by imagined inabilities, why not indulge in a little therapeutic parody?

Chapter Four

How to Begin

1. *Hook and Bounce*

An effective short story is one that hooks us with the first sentence and keeps us reading until the end. A great short story is one that makes us feel that the effort was worthwhile.

This ability to hook the reader is the first requirement of good writing. As Forster says, 'For me, the whole intricate problem of method resolves itself . . . into the power of the writer to bounce the reader into accepting what he says.'

First we hook and then we bounce. These are violent images and they suggest, to the beginner at least, that the style should be sharp.

An opening sentence should suggest one of three things. It may achieve all of them, but it should at least manage one:

a. *Something of moment is about to happen or is already happening*:

There was not an inch of room for Lottie and Kezia in the buggy.
(Katherine Mansfield Prelude)

'You got three quarters of an hour,' said the porter.
(Katherine Mansfield The Journey to Bruges)

If I remember rightly, I have now and then mentioned Paul Masson, known as Lemice-Terieux on account of his delight — and his dangerous efficiency — in creating mysteries.

(Colette The Kepi)

The child who was going to die wanted to hoist himself a little higher against his big pillow but he could not manage it.

(Colette The Sick Child)

The first time I robbed Tiffany's it was raining.
(John Cheever Montraldo)

My father lost me to The Beast at cards.
(Angela Carter The Tiger's Bride)

b. *We are being initiated into a fascinating world*:

Could this ragged girl with brindled lugs have spoken like we do she would have called herself a wolf, but she cannot speak, although she howls when she is lonely . . .
(Angela Carter Wolf-Alice)

Sometimes he thought about his wife, but a thing had begun of late, usually after the boy went to bed, a thing which should have been terrifying but which was not . . .
(James Purdy Colour of Darkness)

You aren't the first man to ask me what I am doing so long in the phone-booth with the door to my flat open and all.
(James Purdy Daddy Wolf)

From the beginning of summer until it seemed pointless, we lifted the thin mattress on to the heavy oak table and made love in front of the large open window.
(Ian McEwan First Love, Last Rites)

Inside the Maison Blondell the steam was so thick that Mrs Watkins felt the tears gathering as she leaned over the client's hand.

(Roland Starke Lionel)

Well, I mean, anything was better than school dinners with the crummy staff at this one.

41

'Oh,' she half laughed, afterwards, each time, 'a teacher, too!'

(B. S. Johnson *On Supply*)

This has the added spice of being a trick beginning, because it suggests that Johnson's aberrant peripatetic is having an elicit affair with a schoolgirl.

c. *We are suspending our need for a and b because this writer is so engagingly witty*:

Arlington Stringham made a joke in the House of Commons. It was a thin House, and a very thin joke; something about the Anglo-Saxon race having a great many angles. It is possible that it was unintentional, but a fellow-member, who did not wish it to be supposed he was asleep because his eyes were shut, laughed. One or two of the papers noted 'a laugh' in brackets, and another, which was careless with its political news, mentioned 'laughter'. Things often begin in that way.

'Arlington made a joke in the House last night,' said Eleanor Stringham to her mother; 'in all of the years we've been married neither of us has made jokes, and I don't like it now. I'm afraid it's a rift in the lute.'

'What lute?' said her mother.

'It's a quotation,' said Eleanor.

To say that anything was a quotation was an excellent method, in Eleanor's eyes, for withdrawing it from discussion, just as you could always defend indifferent lamb late in the season by saying, 'It's mutton.'

(Saki *The Jesting of Arlington Stringham*)

Even if the writing is not witty, it can arrest us by being merely preposterous, as here in my *Absent Fathers*:

'My Mother says my Father is on an expedition up the Amazon,' the very small boy said. 'If he is, then the piranhas must have eaten him,' he added after a decent pause. 'That's what I tell her, and she doesn't contradict me. It's rough having a father you never see, and rougher still having one you've never seen. I only wish she could be a little more inventive concerning his whereabouts, for my sake if not for her own. What about the Lubianka, for example? Or inside a polar bear? A parent like that could last me into my teens — longer in the case of the polar bear.' He smiled, then added bravely, 'She's got a lovely smile, my Mother; but every time she talks of my Father I hear rubber gloves and detect the glitter of test-tubes and syringes. Also she never says "Daddy", never even gives the poor man a name. All she keeps on saying is I must thank God for my polysyllables. She says my Father would have chopped them off long ago if he had been around to hear me prattle. She says she hates vocabulary.'

'And your syntax,' the even smaller girl observed. 'We both deploy a truly remarkable syntax. I've noticed it ever since we met.'

There are two more simple devices for getting a story away to a lively start. One is to devise an arresting title. The other is to be bizarre, though apt, in the choice of characters' names.

Saki's characters include Van Cheele, Blenkinthrop, Mr Attray, Dowager Lady Beanford, Jane Thopplestance, Emma Ladbruk, Dora Bittholtz and Mr Penricarde. His titles range from the abbreviated — *The Unrest Cure*, *The Stalled Ox*, or *Mr. Pacletide's Tiger* — to the substantial mouthful: *Filboid Studge* — *The Story of a Mouse that helped*, *The Peace of Mowsle Barton*, *The Schartz-Metterklume Method*, *The Disappearance of Crispina Umberleigh* or *The Remoulding of Groby Lington*.

Nor are all of his stories jokes. *Shredni Vashtar* is about a small boy who sacrifices his hated shortsighted aunt to his ferret.

Ah, we can object, none of these writers is consistently away to a fine beginning! True, and nor need we be once we have established a long term confidence in a body of readers.

2. *A quick vibration*

So each of our sentences at the beginning of a story needs to strike home. Not only must it be a conscious attempt to captivate, intrigue or annoy our readers: it must tell them what sort of story we are giving them. Is it serious or comic, a genre story or something which seeks to occupy the high ground of fiction? And which of our own categories does it fall into? Angela Carter is always quick to let us know whether we are in the realms of ornate fantasy or political realism.

So, the early words of any piece of fiction are part of a social contract: we are trying to present our work with an appropriate label and in the right package, and a little of it should appear to hang out of the box. To be thus deliberate can help us forward if we advance whole-heartedly. It is easier to think of ourselves as salesmen rather than apostles of high art. We are knocking on someone's door with a trayful of beguiling boxes: we are not offering an abstraction like roof-insulation.

Given this degree of clear-mindedness, we can allow ourselves to run on a bit. It need not all be done by the first sentence alone — or not quite alone:

'This time,' she smiled, 'it will really be for keeps.'

We should be in the realms of high corn; but we know we are not, because the story is called *Suicide Pact*.

Then, too, our opening sentences can blend together like scotch and soda. Providing we don't pour too much before we add the spirit we can get away with putting the water in first:

'A wide shallow pan, lots and lots of sugar, and of course only the very best fruit,' she smiled.
'Do you always make marmalade in a bikini?'

or:

'The Paxton-Smiths have asked us for dinner,' she shouted. 'You know, the new people in that big house on the corner. Black tie, of course.'
'Good,' he smiled. 'I'll pack my bag of tools.'

44

In both cases the game is to wind up the reader; and this can be done with a fair degree of ambiguity:

> She set the razor down carefully, ran herself a hot, deep bath, and waited for the phone to ring.
> Her heart wasn't bleeding yet.

3. *Broadloom takes longer*

I think we've all got the point.

Obviously the beginning of a story lasts longer than the opening sentences. We are going to grab the reader, but we don't want to squeeze him to death. We have to coax things along until there is a fresh injection of interest, and this may not be until the plot meets some point of complication. In a simple linear the story is beginning until it reaches the impediment.

So we try to let out information a bit at a time. The reader wants to come along with us, but he need not be told where he is going, or not exactly.

> 'I hope you don't mind,' he said, 'but I borrowed your place for a couple of hours last night.'
> 'What on earth for?'
> 'I needed to take a girl somewhere. I hope you don't mind.'
> 'I scarcely know you, do I? And I certainly don't know any girl.'
> 'I take it you haven't been back yet,' he said. 'I hope you don't mind, but she broke your coffee pot.'
> 'Which one?'
> 'The green and gold thing I gave you. I hope you don't mind. It was only a cheap one.'
> 'Look,' I said slowly. 'I let you have that key, in an emergency, about a year ago —'
> 'Your emergency,' he smiled.
> 'And my key. I'd like it back, please.'
> 'I don't think I've got it,' he said. 'I let Jemma have it. I hope you don't mind, but she wanted to replace your coffee pot.'

'Jemma's your girlfriend?'

'No, but she's the girl I was with last night. You're not jealous, are you?'

A lot is made of the repetition. It is presumably going to lead up to something quite awful.

The realization that the narrator is a woman is a gradual one, as is the feeling that there is more between the two speakers than meets the eye.

The actual narrative is so sparse that we don't yet know whether it will all be in speech. Our narrator repeats 'he said' more than is strictly necessary, implying some kind of matching mania in herself.

'Jemma' is hardly the usual spelling of the girl's name, yet it is impossible to bandy spellings about in an exchange of direct speech. It depends on our own philosophy of fiction.

'Jemma' is important to us because of its memorable oddness. Dickens knew that nothing fixed a character more firmly than an unusual name, or an unusual spelling of a usual one.

Question: where are these two characters talking? This is not relevant for the moment, though it might become so. What is important is that the story had to begin in the right place. Contrast:

I was just leaving Woolworth's when I bumped into Bobby Smith. I used to know Bobby rather well about a year ago, but I hadn't seen much of Bobby lately, though I'd thought about him.

'I hope you don't mind,' he said, 'but I borrowed your place for a couple of hours last night . . .'

There are arguments in favour of that beginning, but it immediately becomes a different story with less to intrigue the reader.

The problem now is to decide whether we need such a paragraph later in the story (at the point we have reached in version number one, with a suitable change of tense?) or whether it is best left out altogether. Wherever we put it will profoundly influence the feel of the writing.

46

This is not a duplex. Someone is telling us *her* story. Whether or not Jemma is anything more than a ghost character, we still have an important question to ask the narrator: 'Where were *you* last night?'

Do we need to know how our story will end at this point? Preferably, but not necessarily. When it has ended we shall have to make certain that it still has the right beginning.

This isn't angel cake, is it?

Angel cake may help us solve a problem or two, but not very tidily. Suppose we decide that the whole story so far has been told by the narrator to a friend:

> Romy Dexter still hadn't come up with that glass of gin. 'I can't think why you let that little tick buy you presents,' she said slowly. 'And as for letting him get his hands on your key . . .'

4. *Tighter string*

So far the various examples of duplex I have scattered about have been slow-moving beginner's fare. Duplex can be extremely brisk:

> 'With a man like that you want to move fast,' Fiona Hunt said to Josie Auerbach.
>
> 'I have moved fast. I married him last Easter.'
>
> 'You want to keep *him* moving,' Fiona explained. 'That way the vultures won't get him.'
>
> 'What vultures?'
>
> 'Me for one.'

This is clearly not Fiona's story only. Josie is much too combative for this to be angel cake. In the next example, we are not so sure. The Aunt may be no more than a destructive chorus to the main action. But if this *is* angel cake, it certainly crumbles fast:

> 'Marrying Jennifer is going to be idyllic,' Howard said to his Aunt. 'It is going to be like an endless holiday on a desert island.'

'She does have a rather dry skin,' his Aunt admitted, 'and an even drier cough. Tell me about some of her other attributes.'

'Perhaps I meant treasure island.'

'That was never in question, surely?'

We already know quite a lot about both characters, and can sense a thing or two about the luckless Jennifer. The story is well begun without being committed in any direction.

5. *A little more rain and Roberta*

It is always reassuring to discover how other people start their stories and to explore some of their options, and even more heartening to realize that they ever manage to start at all. Suppose we are stuck?

If we are stuck *with* an idea, then I am afraid there is no alternative but to try all of the possible beginnings page-top by page-top until the correct one presents itself. Does it commence with character, circumstance or event? Can we pack all three into a brief unlumpish sentence? Shall we take one at a time? Will angel cake and the prop of a fictional audience help? Is the story contained in a document?

Generally when we are stuck, we are stuck *without* a story. This is as true now as it was in Chapter One. All we can do is consult our notebooks and expand on a fragment or play pass-the-parcel. We can even combine the two.

Suppose I have jotted down my Rob and Roberta nonsense (p. 37), and it now represents the sum total of my investment? I must contrive some sort of relationship between myself and the material and then between the material and my reader, however coy and frail such an overture seems.

Once I have truly begun, I can prune and discard. For the moment, to make things easy, I am going to include everything, even my doubts and self-mockery. They will provide me with a stance and perhaps the necessary narrative demotic:

It was raining.

I was on the way to see Rob in the Fiat Dad had bought me.

Rob used to be my friend but she wasn't now. (Rob short for Roberta. Everything was short for Rob. You can tell the effect she had on me. I am telling this the way we talked to each other, as if we were in a short story by Hemingway).

The Fiat was misbehaving. Its engine was full of warm Italian blood, and it didn't like the wet. The screen wipers were beginning to go spastic, and in a minute I knew I should have to stop the car, lift the bonnet and tighten that greasy little nut that fastens the whole bloody jigsaw to the works . . .

I have put everything in, all as it strikes me. This has provided me with a style, and the style is smoothing itself down and becoming viable. Of course I shall edit it, but not until I know more about my narrator's character and tone of voice. Last time Roberta's ex-friend was a woman: is this the same friend?

Such as it is, the story has begun. Depression, frustration and perhaps mania lurk in the over-chirpy style. More important, the Fiat is its own kind of Bloody Great Wheel and it is rolling. Event is looming at least insofar as the narrator has to stop the car and stand all alone in the manically downfalling rain and put his or her head into the engine with the leaves hurrying past, water sogging the legs, and the torch not quite adequate and —

Is the narrator alone? Is Granny there? Is Roberta's child, or the Alsatian, chained up on the back seat?

There is a beginning, *on paper*. Now is the time to walk round the block.

Chapter Five

What Comes Next?

1. *Bulging Bellies and Trim Waists*

Most people can manage to start a story. The problem is to
carry it on.

The first thing to realize is that every piece of writing
grinds to a halt somewhere. We need to give ourselves time,
a month even, so that when we come back to it we can read
it with fresh eyes and full attention:

> The cigarette had lasted Minni Hoep for several hours. It
> survived because she hadn't lit it. When its filter became
> too damp or too soiled she would throw it away and not
> light another one. She hated the smell of cigarettes, the
> taste of their smoke, what they did to her breath and her
> armpits. But her purple cat-suit, her mauve boots, belt and
> eyelids needed a long cigarette worn at a dangerous angle.
> The cigarette demonstrated the way she felt about herself;
> and when she understood just what that was she would do
> without it.

All we have so far is a moderately interesting character, with
only the slowly moistening cigarette offering any indication
of passing time. We obviously can't think of a linear, or we
should get on with it (though why Minni can't buy a cup of
tea or catch a bus escapes me for the present); so we shall

comb our notebook or our hair for a duplex — another character to bounce her against.

Minni's friend Sher was not sucking a cigarette. She had a finger-end in her mouth, and both mouth and finger had been specially groomed for the purpose. She had studied the benefits her finger could confer on her face a long long time in her bedroom mirror. She knew just what it suggested when it hung from its painted and specially elongated nail, and how the sense of danger increased when she gnawed it by the knuckle. Sometimes she chewed on its ring, sometimes its glove. The effect was limited but magical. She looked as if she was shortly to burst out laughing, announce her engagement to a member of the Royal Family or suffer an epileptic fit. She was, in short, a perfect companion for a girl with an unlit cigarette.

We don't have to go back to Minni yet. Just that little sentence at the end will do. If we bounce the reader's attention too swiftly to-and-fro we shall induce a kind of Wimbledon exhaustion.

Sher wore her school uniform, the all navy blue one with the navy blue shoes, navy blue tunic, navy blue hat and the black tights. While she was at school she refused to have a school uniform in the house; but the moment she left she had seen how well one would look standing next to a purple cat suit and mauve boots, so she had bought three, and lots and lots of black tights; and she had grown a long finger nail.

We still can't find a plot, but we have a highly exploitable duo. They are still workable in duplex.

Minni — Minni with an i — Minni Hoep was obviously a German name, or Dutch, or just possibly Polish. It stood out a mile because it was certainly foreign, and even more than that because it was so ugly. She said it was pronounced Hoop, but Hoop with two syllables, as if it was a hoop being rolled by a Geordie. 'Say Hoo-oop,' she

51

used to say to people. 'It comes more easily if you think of it with a W in front of it, just like a Red Indian war cry or the baby's cough. "Who-oop!" — try that!' Trying it used to embarrass strangers for hours; but it meant that Minni was never short of something to talk about. They used to play this trick a long way from home, so only Minni — and, of course, Sher — knew her real name was Hope, and that she had turned herself into a mystery by the bold transposition of two little letters.

The duplex is working well, but to the bizarre characterization has been added an unmistakable hint of danger. The girls talk to strangers, spend hours playing tricks on them. 'Mystery' suggests trouble. The word has been planted. It is hoods' slang for girls who leave home too young and are tricked on to the street.

The beauty of duplex construction is that it need only last as long as we want it to. Danger implies impediment. A plot is beginning to suggest itself, and it could be a simple linear. For example, the girls share a single obsession and pursue it in the face of a shared impediment.

Actually, I think not. The idea of two girls placing themselves separately at risk while maintaining a high degree of insouciance is so attractive that it will be best to carry on juxtaposing their circumstances, rather than involve them in the same mess.

The relationship between duplex and linear does not always offer so many ambiguities:

Marcus had a new wife so he never took his teeth out. They took themselves out sometimes when he was drunk; and once they even bit him, but his new wife was sleeping in a warm layer of huff in the next room so she did not catch him lying with his bottom set in his shoulderblade and his top set in his bottom, and that perhaps was as well.

So far we only have the glimmerings of a duplex. We do have a man with a wife (and linear enthusiasts might well say that this is impediment enough). The duplex is deployed either to help us to carry the story forward or because the narrative has started the wrong way round; in other words, the focus should be on the wife but the teeth are too good to pass over:

> His new wife's name was Mary, and she was well aware he had teeth. Wives know most things about their husbands, and about other women's husbands as well, especially when they try to conceal them. Teeth are almost impossible to hide, not least when you are doing old-fashioned things with them like eating or laughing or filtering air. Marcus did most of these at some time or other, so Mary only had to wait and she would catch him.

Now we know what the story is about. If the plot is to be a game of evasion — Mary stalks, Marcus continues to camouflage — then the duplex will be the best strategy. This chopping and changing between character and character is well suited to comedy, because comedy likes to be objective.

But most good duplex plots suggest opposing linears. Mary wishes, for whatever reason, to expose her husband as a wearer of dentures (impediment: husband's obduracy); Marcus wishes to conceal from his wife, again for whatever reason, his dependence on the dentist (impediment: his wife's determined watchfulness). The short story could equally well continue by favouring a single linear and presenting one character as the comic hero and the other as the comic villain. In this case, the opening duplex is not wasted. It is a very economic way of introducing the reader to the impediment.

I cannot imagine ever getting stuck in a story like this (as Saki's Unbearable Bassington so aptly observes, 'It is all a question of knowing exactly how far to go, and then going one step farther'), but angel cake is always on hand to sustain us. This could be especially good here, because the moment we turn to a narrator we have to ask who it should be and what role he should play; and the obvious narrator here is the dentist, especially if he ministers to Mary as well as to Marcus.

Sher was summoned to help Minni, and Mary to hound Marcus, not because the duplex is closest to my theory of fiction — it is not — but because Sher and Mary *by their presence* move the imagination forward. Writing turns upon tiny ideas. We need to find them, then piece them together. The duplex does both of these things supremely well. It generally makes for plumper, slower narrative than the linear; but it is reassuringly simple to write on a bad day.

For example, in the last chapter I introduced a very small fatherless boy (p. 42). Even in my most dufferish mood I was able to contrive an even smaller girl. The only real choice was to decide whether she too was fatherless. The texture of the writing more or less compelled me to make her as precocious of speech as he was. It is only now, after much hindsight, that I see that equal fun could have been obtained by having her say nothing (turn her into angel cake perhaps?) or hover on the fringes of goo-goo and ga-ga (a difficult technical problem). Anyway, I gave her a speech that in every respect outdoes his, and then decided to answer the question that so obviously puts itself:

He was about seven years old and she was a very mature six, and both of them were so lost in envy and self-admiration that they let a decent silence settle before the little girl said, 'I very much doubt that rubber gloves story of yours.'

'I've discussed it with my analyst. She says it's a very reasonable anxiety and not the least neurotic. She tells me that test-tubes and syringes make some of the best fathers, or some of the least complicated anyway, and she advises me not to fret myself about it. She says there are lots of grown women who can't stand having grown men around, and are altogether happier without them.'

'My therapist says it's because grown men are always such little boys,' the girl said inconsequentially. 'Didn't yours really suggest you might be barking up the wrong tree with all that rubber glove stuff? Mine told me I'd be far better off facing the fact that I was probably the result of some alcoholic slap-and-tickle after an office party.'

'My Mother doesn't work in an office,' the little boy said.

'Perhaps you were adopted.'

'Mother's shown me the scar.'

'Mummy doesn't have a scar.'

'Perhaps you were adopted.'

'She says I came out the usual way.'

'I think that's disgusting. I'd far rather come out through a scar. My analyst says my Mother will say the scar shows how much she cares for me, and I'm not to take any notice of her when she tells me because it will be a petty piece of emotional blackmail.'

'How brave of you.'

'Mother hasn't said it yet.'

'My therapist says I mustn't grow up thinking sex is unwholesome and furtive because Mummy never had any except in my case, and then only unwholesome and furtive sex, whatever that might be.'

'That's a subjunctive,' the little boy said. 'By the way, I've been meaning to ask someone this, but what's the difference between an analyst and a therapist?'

'About six guineas an hour,' the little girl said grandly ...

The duplex works very well, even though nothing much has happened. Nor does anything need to happen, because a little reflection will suggest that it is a conversation piece.

It needs reworking. If the children are to have no names, then the no-names must be consistent. One must stay as 'the very small boy' and the other, just possibly, continue to be 'the even smaller girl' — not as here. Their speech could be archer. After all, the whole thing is already way over the top. The problem is to keep it there.

2. *Paper tigers*

The duplex is for on-the-page thinkers. It forms the basis of much meaningful exercise and a considerable body of finished writing.

It is equally possible to doodle a linear, but the revision stage will need to be extremely strict to prevent flaccid development. In truth, I have never constructed 'a paper linear' without reaching the moment when I knew it would have to be entirely rewritten. The best that can be said is that doodling has filled an empty head with a plot.

Tyros should look for linears that encourage the reader to meet them halfway. We are always interested in the progress of a love story, a hijack, an escape, or the outcome of a conflict or a competition (they are all versions of the Bloody Great Wheel, and it is now, mid-story, that we can congratulate ourself if we have one rolling). A man taking on thirty pints of beer is a never failing source of inspiration, and a slim girl with clear unwatery eyes and up-market profile similarly embattled is good enough for a title story. Advanced practitioners will take it at a page a pint for five pints, and pack the other twenty-five into a frothy sentence. The Grand Master's decision is to select the right five pints.

One of the attractions of this sort of story is that while we can all understand the action we can never fathom the motive or the psychological outcome.

In other words, we are interested in anyone who plays with fire. It is the duty of the writer to ensure that, in the middle of the story and for as long as possible thereafter, the man who dines on hot coals does not get burnt, nor the sword-swallower puncture his gizzard. In Chapter Four I quoted a B. S. Johnson beginning — a first person narrative by a schoolmaster who appeared to be involved with a schoolgirl (p. 41). In fact he is not. He is having lunchtime sex (and frozen food) with the girl's mother. The girl is a delinquent, and so is the mother. He knows that this can't last, that he will soon be kicked out of bed and school. What keeps him interesting is that, although he knows he is everyone's victim, he doesn't care. As he says, it's better than school dinners.

3. *A timely helping of cake*

No matter how clear a linear seems to be to us, it is crucial that we understand what is happening sentence by sentence. A good linear reaches back to oral beginnings. It is supposed to be a yarn that spins itself. That is the terrible danger of it.

Here is a first draft of a short story about an international kidnap.

The customs boys were very thorough.

They checked the patient to make sure his wheelchair wasn't bristling with contraband; then the officers at the passport desk were curious enough to nudge them into searching the sick man's luggage. Perfect. He had a case filled with dirty laundry, all wrapped up in polythene bags, and a case packed with clean stuff and all the usuals, including photographs of him with his alleged wife and kids.

It is important to recognize this for what it is, a fast moving but choric beginning that summarizes events that occurred before the main action opened. It needs to be made sense of quickly. What better than to capitalize on the slight element of angel cake, the omniscient narrator suggested by the word 'alleged', and convert it to interrogation and report?

Direct speech is a necessary ingredient of real action:

'He was actually in these photographs?'

'Yes. They're easy enough to fake.'

'You showed all of these lads the genuine mugshots?'

'Yes, indeed. It was Kay right enough. And Kay in the family snaps. Him or the chap he's being mistaken for.'

I should have known their procedures would be impeccable. The only problem was where did it leave me? Worse, much worse: where did it leave Charles Augustus Kay? He had been smuggled out of the country in circumstances that made it unlikely anyone would ever put him back.

The interior monologue is now bang up-to-date, and the soggy but very necessary opening summary has been suitably enhanced. The linear is well underway.

57

One last point. This is a two person story, but it would fail horribly as a duplex. Hide and seek, hunter and hunted, are much better followed from a single viewpoint. Whenever there is restless action, the duplex will slow it down. Nor will a multi-viewpoint single strand narrative work in this case. Only a novel has enough space for that. The two men are not riding the same wheel.

Chapter Six

Dying and Rising Falls

1. *Decent endings*

Short stories do not need to dispense profundity. The better a story fits its skin the more meaningful it will be seen to be. As Chekhov once said in a letter, Art has to ask the right questions, not set out to answer them. Far better to finger a nerve than batter the brain.

The first thing about finishing a story is to get out of it quickly. Both of the David Pownall endings quoted in Chapter Two (p. 20-22) are extremely brisk. He *accelerates* out. The necessary reflective note at the end of *Hump MacBride and Suicide* is induced by a single image. By the end of the story the reader's imagination should be meeting the writer halfway.

The short story can achieve this most easily if it appears to select from life rather than reshape or recreate it. The narrative breaks off, but life — and the characters the story has just revealed to us — still goes on. Indeed, the very best ending is often to suggest that there is a further unrevealed instalment. In the B. S. Johnson story about the school-master, the narrator withdraws from love but leaves the school and its uneaten dinners quite explicitly in place. He also leaves us with the roguish suggestion that he has been supplanted as a lover by the headmaster.

So if the linear ends with a twist, it must impart its final information as deftly as possible. The woman in de Maupassant's *The Necklace* discovers *in a sentence* that she and her husband have wasted their entire lives toiling to repay a non-existent debt. Because this is *fresh* information it has to be entirely reasonable, and in keeping with the rest of the story. Rich people do sometimes wear pastework copies of jewellery too expensive to risk out of the safe. We all know this. It is both a truth and a literary convention. It does not have to be explained to us. If it did, there would be no story.

It is better still, if the story contains all of its own information. In Mayne-Reid's famous slab of angel cake we know all along that the Guyas Gutas does not exist. If it does, it is certainly not inside the hero's packing-case: he has told us so. We also know that *did* this beast exist it would be hideously ferocious. We read on simply to discover how the narrator and his friend are going to escape from a theatre filled with people who have paid them money to have the wild animal displayed before them. The growls seem authentic, so does the rattle of chain, the pawing of woodwork behind the curtain. The moment of truth has to pass quickly, again in the space of a sentence. The hero staggers before us covered in gore and exclaims in a hoarse voice, 'Gentlemen! the Guyas Gutas has escaped. Save your wives and your children!'

This story and the B. S. Johnson are really versions of the sword of Damocles. The blade is suspended above someone's head and we read breathlessly to the end to discover whether or not it will fall. In one case it does: not in the other. The device works either way.

In a duplex construction, the symmetry is not disturbed if the blade hangs unseen by everyone, including the reader. However contemptuous Aristotle may be of the *deus ex machina* in a classical tragedy we all know that real life abounds with unsuspected alternatives, especially alternatives of disaster. It becomes bad art only if the shape of events is wrong. In a linear, we feel cheated by an external solution. Not in a duplex. The Wolf and the Bear have their set-piece squabble over the chicken. Meanwhile the Fox steals it.

Foxes are like that. The third party need not represent a higher reality for us to be morally and aesthetically satisfied, merely a *realer* one.

Here is a stalled duplex that is admirably solved by such a trivial device:

The minute Jessica saw Bill she knew she had to have him. 'It's a superior kind of psychic attractiveness,' she confessed to Josephine, her best friend. 'It goes beyond passion, and it certainly goes beyond trousers. I suppose I shall have to marry him or something, simply because I need to see a certain amount of him day by day, week by week, until the moment I die, when we shall quite certainly meld on a Higher Plane. I wish you could see his aura. It's whiter than Kether in Aziluth.'

'It's his bank balance,' Josephine said. 'And all of the family oil. He's the four hundred and thirty-first richest man in the world and you should see his list of director-ships — longer than a python's tail. I've looked him up, you see. I've done my homework and I have to tell you you are aeons too late. I don't mind if he marries me, divorces me with a vast alimony or simply sends me flowers, provided he sets me up in one of those little fifteen bedroom places on St Anne's Hill. It would be so good for my asthma.'

This is another talking piece, but the conversation is always after bizarre incident and against exotic — not to say esoteric — background; and, as with all life and most art, time passes:

The friends' obsession with Bill did not abate; and it says much for their relationship that they were able to discuss progress, compare notes and even lay bets. Sometimes Jessica drew ahead, sometimes Josephine, both of them getting nearer in turn until it was clear to each of them that one day soon she would do as she had always intended and have Bill.

Renata already had him. She had had him for some

time. She did not notice the two friends, and saw to it that Bill didn't either.

Plots cannot all end in frustration. The foiled linear and the twist are all very well, but they are hard to devise and philosophically questionable. If each of our stories had a sting in the tail our readers would quickly become immune to the poison.

People do quite often win through, so there is no reason why a linear should not end happily. All it needs is a quick pull of focus:

'Yes,' she said quickly, 'the treatment really works. My last scan was clear.' She caught me by the arm. 'It's your turn now.'

Or perhaps the ending is not as bright as all that? We should always be careful about qualifying 'said'. So late in a story shorthand sets in. That 'quickly' carries an awful lot of weight.

If the narrator and the protagonist remain in a separate category, the result will have the right ring of truth. Everyone's linear does not always end in a crock of gold:

There could only be one reason for entering a car park.
'I've saved for a deposit. I'm really quite pleased with it.'
Pauline had got what she wanted at last. I never did.

At the end of a story, narrator and protagonist often do draw apart like this. The writer, as so often, has to resort to a tiny crumb of angel cake.

2. *More than a crumb*

As I said two chapters ago, the cake is always waiting. The problem is to find out where it is. It is always handy at the close of a story. How soon do we need to bring it in?

Not until we need to. Forster wrote scathingly of primitives by the fire. One of them has a story to tell, and for the moment there are dark reasons for making it a dull one. It would be very foolish indeed to make it even duller by including his audience.

In summary: when he woke this morning he stretched and scratched, went behind the tree, untangled his beard, breakfasted on the remains of the meat, walked to the stream, loitered back again, marched right up across the hill and over the next one, sat in the shade of a tall rock, moved round it as the sun moved, ate a few nuts, slept for a while, was fortunate enough to wake up again, remembered to stand up, felt his way back over the second hill and was reassured the near hill was right where he had left it this morning, so now here he is, and now we need the angel cake.

This man's recital will doubtless bring comfort to his tribe and pass a little time between dusk and darkness; but they won't clamour to hear him retell it.

They want to hear the story the old woman has just told. They want to hear it over and over again.

How she went to wash in the stream and came face to face with a bear that was wading for fish. How she didn't run or scream. How the bear didn't tear her face off, but simply handed her a salmon.

'Tell us again about you and the bear and the salmon,' they'll say. And she will tell them again and again.

'That reminds me,' our historian geographer says. 'It quite slipped my mind till this minute, but now I come to think of it, I met a bear myself today. It was probably the same bear because it was wet round the wrists and ankles, and it had a damp nose when it kissed me.'

'Tell us.'

'I told you how I sat in the shade of a tall rock, then moved as the sun moved. But then I fell asleep. When I woke I was still in the shade. It was the shade of the bear.'

The important matter to grasp is that the angel cake has to be kept out for as long as possible, but at the same time introduced well before the end. Direct speech is the best way of reporting dialogue but the worst way to convey action.

3. *Black Dogs*

Tales of the occult and supernatural seem to obey different rules. It is an accepted part of the tradition that the supernatural begins with a story within a story, with a warning offered or a warning withheld; and almost a convention that this should be given by a publican, a retreating stranger, a fey child, an eminent but derided occultist or a girl with green eyes; sometimes — and not in self-parody — by a melange of the lot of them.

Sometimes the angel cake is discarded early:

> Traveller listens to barman's tale about weird doings up at the Grange.
> Traveller goes to the Grange in clear narrative and does not report back to the barman, perhaps because he is dead. (We know there are toothmarks on his neck, so we don't need the barman to tell us).

Just as often the traveller does report back, and the barman uncovers some extra twist in the story.

> Barman: Do not walk in the Park between sunset and sunrise. Tonight is the Night of the Wolf.
> Traveller goes out and returns.
> Traveller: I have traversed the Park even as far as the Grange.
> Barman: Then you must have encountered the Fenris Wolf.
> Traveller: I met a dog as big as a horse, but he did me no harm.
> Barman: Then what is that hole in your neck?

The reader knows that the traveller met the wolf and fought with him. The reader does not know he is injured or — as so often in this genre — one of the walking dead. Disguised in

64

the angel cake we have a simple linear with twist. The strange fact is that a fictional audience can impart fresh information right at the end of the story, and not have its author struck off the register.

A student of mine on a writing weekend wrote an excellent Black Dog story in which herself as narrator and another woman go scrambling about the screes in spite of a warning from the ubiquitous barman. The Black Dog confronts them in a gully. They run and are separated. She returns to the pub to look for her friend, but the barman comes up with a final piece of lore: the Black Dog never appears without killing someone.

Chapter Seven

Painless Revision

1. *Not a spade but a literate shovel*

A writer must be literate. He may come to argue with editors about the merits of 'into' as against 'in to'; and with printers who want characters to say, 'I am 27 years old,' instead of 'I am twenty seven years old'; and with newspaper and magazine subs who insist that 'twenty nine' and all numbers below are written as words, whatever the circumstance; and '30' and all numbers above are written as figures. House rules may be as horrible to him as a jammed typewriter; but at the centre of all of his debates — with himself, with his muse, with his style, with his publisher, his critics and his audience — must be the conviction that he is writing good English. His stories may abound with dialect and be narrated in some esoteric demotic, but he has to be confident that his practice is based on sound conventional grammar.

Most people who read this are hideously illiterate. Language is not well taught in school, and few of us are motivated to absorb what is on offer until it is much too late. Well, a writer just has to learn to write; and writing is the simplest way to learn.

A dictionary should always be within reach of the desk. *Collins Dictionary of the English Language* (1979) is the best general lexicon on the market; and *The Oxford Illustrated Dictionary* (second edition) is useful for the definition of words hard to visualize, such as ketch, plinth, glacis, arquebus and pedunculate. Thereafter our library can enlarge to suit our needs. A good thesaurus is useful, so that we can browse and find alternative words. Any impression of the 1962 edition of *Roget* is good. The 1981 edition is a minefield: it was revised by an ideologue and some of its entries are plain daft.

Grammar books are to be avoided. So are dons and schoolteachers. I have been both, but I always switch myself off when I start to write. The intending writer who is seriously in doubt about his literacy must do three things: press on regardless; write parodies of the great; read the next page or two with absolute attention.

2. *Minimum grammar*

This is how to spell, how to write and punctuate the simple sentence and paragraph, how to recognize and punctuate direct speech.

All people spell more or less well or more or less badly according to whether they are optimists or pessimists. Spelling is done by the dictionary, so bad spelling is lazy and ill-mannered. That being said, I must admit to having words jump from my typewriter that I have never put in to it, and occasionally to going boss-eyed in front of a piece of paper because I cannot shake the correct sequence of letters from my pen. Pessimists like myself should compile a list of all the words that make them wake up gnashing their teeth at night. Even the most grubby practitioners will probably find that they misspell no more than a hundred words. A hundred words is an unusually long list. It should be corrected and learned by heart. Optimists will know at once that even twenty words will plug an appalling gap in the ego.

The act of reading another author closely enough to parody him will probably teach what a sentence is. It will certainly teach what a sentence by that author is. Parody, and grovelling admiration, are all that can motivate close enough reading.

However, parody is not for everyone. Do not waste time

with definitions. 'A sentence is a group of words that makes complete sense' I was taught. I can think of all manner of groups of words and even single words that make complete sense yet are not sentences, and so can everyone else: words like 'Ladies' Cloakroom', 'Danger!' and 'Last Exit to Brooklyn'. The only way to learn to write and punctuate sentences is to understand verbs. Learn that verbs are the doing or being words in any collection, become familiar with them all so you can recognize them like long lost lovers as they go flashing past the speeding window of your prose. There a verb, and there a verb, and there a verb, so you pull the communication cord and summon the guard. Verbs need to travel closely accompanied by a full stop. If they cannot produce a full stop within the space of a dozen syllables or so, you should produce one for them with a brisk editorial flourish. They may offer to buy you off with a *connecting* word, a relative pronoun such as 'who' or 'which', a so-called relative adverb such as 'when' or 'where', a conjunction such as 'and' and 'but' or a conjunctive adverb such as 'while', any of which can be used to cobble little sentences into bigger and bigger sentences. It is a waste of time to learn to separate their functions. There are very few such words, say a dozen, and they can be learned. Do not give them too much use. Short sentences are best in narrative. Confidence will come with a liberal application of the full stop. Everything else will follow.

Example: I kissed her she punched me on the nose.

'Kissed' and 'punched' are obviously *doing* words. It is clear what words belong to 'kiss' and what words belong to 'punch', so the full stop and capital letter drop into place:

I kissed her. She punched me on the nose.

Or we can join the sentences with an appropriate link, 'so', 'but' or 'although', even 'as' and 'when'. There is much fun in such tiny syllables:

I kissed her so she punched me on the nose.

Learning to punctuate sentences is a matter of self-editing, then. If something won't edit, chuck it out. Get rid of anything that is rough, defies definition, or that you are not in control of.

To increase the dimension of your self-editing learn to correct as for the printer. *The Writers' and Artists' Yearbook* includes the proof-correction code as well as much useful advice about marketing. A pessimist who corrects himself in this way will feel more like his own publisher and less like his own schoolteacher.

3. *Prose spins on a paragraph*

Sometimes it is easier to run than to walk. The sentences are bound to become easier if work is broken into brief paragraphs. The great slab of prose will not appear so daunting.

How often should there be a new paragraph?

As often as possible.

When should there be a new paragraph?

Whenever there is the least doubt about the matter.

How short can a paragraph be?

As short as the shortest sentence.

How long can a paragraph be?

In theory as long as the ideas cluster together. In fact, narrative should shun long paragraphs. Events are presented in sequence rather than concepts in parallel. We are not dealing with aesthetics but our reader's eyestrain. So if we haven't got at least three paragraphs on a page, we should do something about it for the sake of our audience.

At the start of a narrative, short — even one sentence — paragraphs help to wind up the tension. They also encourage the reader to devour space, and this is important. Short stories are rejected somewhere on page one. Nobody puts a story aside on page two:

Jill was pacing round the room again.

Sooner or later Jack was going to do something about her.

I watched him slump in his chair. He'd been that way for hours.

It was then that I realized something was badly wrong.

This *can* go over the top, but readers are much more tolerant of the brisk and staccato than of the sonorous and never-ending.

There must always be a new paragraph for each change of speaker when direct speech is used, or for a switch from speaker to observer. (Direct speech is, quite simply, a verbatim report of words actually spoken by, or invented for, a character. It is punctuated as the examples indicate):

'Got a light?'

'If this will do.'

I held out the sparkler and watched him try to light his cigarette from it.

'Haven't we met before?'

I didn't answer.

If the speaker finishes speaking and then acts, or acts and then speaks, it is a matter of judgment whether we use a new paragraph or not:

'If this will do.' I held out the sparkler . . .

A sensitive reader, or a reader who has had time to adapt to the pace of this particular story, will sense the slight hesitation implied by the change of paragraph. The 'I' does not react kindly to strangers asking for a light.

Strictly, a change of actor requires a new paragraph:

I held out the sparkler and watched *him try to light his cigarette from it.*

Although 'he' is acting 'I' am watching '*him*' act. He is performing a reported or indirect action. If he performs a direct action, the paragraphing should be like this:

I held out the sparkler.
  He tried to light his cigarette from it.

This is absolutely correct, but the rule can be bent a little (when paragraphing direct speech, the rule is absolute):

I held out the sparkler. He tried to light his cigarette from it.

The motive here might be quite simply that the reader is felt to have had enough staccato. More subtly, it keeps the focus on the narrator. Direct action is being paragraphed as if it is indirect action. The man is not merely lighting a cigarette; he is being closely observed lighting a cigarette.

Of course, language itself can cause us to defy convention. This is impeccable:

I hit him.
  He feinted and ducked under my arm, then began to run towards the perimeter fence.

But it works almost as well like this:

I hit him, but he feinted and ducked under my arm, then began to run towards the perimeter fence.

Let us hope that we are at that developing point in the story when author and reader are in telepathic communion. If not, that little 'but' has a lot of explaining to do. Perhaps it implies 'seen from my point of view he was a pretty elusive chap!'

4. *The Kindest Cut of All*

It will hurt. It always hurts. But when in doubt cut it out. If the narrative is flaccid cut it till it flexes. Initially be very suspicious of adverbs and adjectives. Fiction depends upon exact nouns and appropriate verbs. If three pages become two sentences of ten words apiece, rejoice. Or rejoice if they are two sentences that work.

Do not say 'suddenly'. Find a sudden verb. Or do not find a sudden verb. 'I was suddenly aware' says little more than 'I was aware', and it takes longer and is therefore less sudden. The suddenness will come in the awareness: 'I was aware that he was cocking his pistol' is ten times brisker than 'I was suddenly aware that he was cocking his pistol.' In general, if a proposition's opposite has no meaning, then nor does the proposition itself: 'I was gradually aware that he was cocking his pistol. . . . ?' Treat all adverbs with similar suspicion.

In the same sentence, think about the 'that', think about the 'his'. The one is unnecessary, the other too specific. Pistols are monsters with a separate life. 'I was aware he was cocking the pistol' is much, much better; but other problems begin to present themselves as a result. Do not try to unriddle my conundrums. If you have none of your own, then clearly you will never write.

Sometimes I cut from lack. I cannot make this work. Perhaps, therefore, it is not necessary in the total sum of my world or my world's work. Generally, cutting makes something work. The cut evades the cliché. Impossible always to think of something that is not a cliché, or not boring because no more than expected. So the cut is a kind of resurrection. It resurrects speed, or the reader's awareness:

'Do you love me?'
'No.'
She went on combing the cat.

She could say 'no', she could say 'yes'; she could embark upon some subtle speech of acceptance or rejection that I lack the wit to write. If I write it, it might be a yawn. In fiction, truth is often in error. So, like a coward, I have her say 'No'.

A writer would have her say nothing:

'Do you love me?'
She went on combing the cat.

The cat-combing is, after all, the moment of invention.

In general, people answer too much in beginners' fiction.

'Nice day.'
   'Lovely. I'll have a pint of your best.'

Why not:

'Nice day.'
   'I'll have a pint of your best.'

or:

'Nice day.'
   I couldn't bear to answer the slob. I bought a pint of best and carried it to the corner of the bar.
('carried', 'took', 'walked with it'?)

Again you see the beastly preoccupation! But Chandler has a useful caution here. A writer should be finicky with words, he agrees; but he shouldn't get carried away. The *mot exact* is not always the *mot juste*:

His fingers quibbled with the keys. He watched the cat wince footstep by footstep on the lawn, which still itched with dew.
   Presently Caroline would come, *lorgnette*, *peignoir et al*, and commence her anointing of the aspidistra with rose-water and milk.

5. *So stay out of the mirror*

Don't qualify your narrator's actions, especially his or her speech: 'Yes,' I said curtly, laconically, winsomely, with an engaging smile; this just won't do. Anyone who thinks that it will is spending too much time in front of a tape-recorder or mirror.

It *is* possible to suggest the narrator is a narcissistic

egomaniac, but this needs to be done carefully; and with a bad egg at the front of the box you will find it hard to sell the basket.

Think of the market. It is hard to reach a very careful reader with your modulated signal of deliberate excess, when a moderately careful reader, for example your editor, will conclude on the same evidence that you are merely being sloppy. Besides, careful readers are a tribe invented by dons. Real readers are not careful. They *are* prepared to be creative on the strength of carefully coded clues.

So when we come to revise a story, we should make sure that it begins. We should see that it ends fast, then try to make it faster. As for the rest?

We should put it aside, not for Horace's seven years but for several days. We should revise it, but never for long at a time because we need to decide what is fresh in it, and we can only do this if we are fresh ourselves.

If we are prepared to give ourselves time *away* as well as time *with*, then revision will become easy. Once revision is easy, writing is easy.

Chapter Eight

A Body of Work and How to Sell It

1. *Some things we just can't help*

In the last chapter it became clear, clear as when listening to a lunatic, that concerning style in fiction I entertain certain dangerous obsessions. I shared them, but did not seek to pass them on. Sooner or later you will be infected with your own. Whatever you come to do in writing, you will have your own ways of doing things. Every word you write from that moment will increase your sense of what you are about. Each new story will break new ground. You will regard it in wonder and be certain it is not yours, that you ought to tear it up, not because it is bad but because it does not conform to the canon. Now is the time to be comforted. Whatever you do, however disnatured, will be closer to yourself than it is to anyone else. Your readers will come to recognize it, your friends in the writing circle will pick it out of the pack. You will have begun to produce a body of work.

This is a pompous term, but it is what we want. We require all of our stories to belong together like a box of cutlery. It is partly a creative imperative and partly a practicality. They will need so to belong if we are to sell them as a book or collect them into a book after we have sold them one by one.

Once we have searched ourselves deeply enough the process will be automatic. Everyone has a style, some of it born of success, most of it on the long retreat from failure. This is not to say that we cannot help it along.

It may be that the short story is only a stepping stone, as it was for Angus Wilson. We will pretty certainly not be as successful with it as he was, but like him we shall turn towards the novel. We may decide to do both, or the story prove to be all we can do.

As I point out in the next chapter, the story by itself is not a very saleable item. For publishers it is an irritating particle. We can cure all this by producing work that clusters to a theme, or better still to some related circumstances. Pickwick began like this, and Pickwick outran the page and set his author up for life.

So I would advise writers to move in two directions, and in one of them very slowly. Of course it is good to explore. We should also learn to exploit.

That story about the school. It was full of beguiling children. There were two really memorable teachers, and the *smell* of the place was just right: fish dinners, wet raincoats and polish. Surely we can use it again? Or if not that one, the one about the hospital ward, the nurses, the members of the club, commuters on the same train, the people on a package tour.

Perhaps all that is too obvious. So too the line-workers, the waiters, the cooks, the factory girls, the people who work in the laundry, the launderette, the service-station, the public parks.

It may be our theme should be mania, poverty, loneliness, dissent in the family.

Or perhaps themes are not for us, but a genre begins to beckon. Detective fiction is rare in the short form today; but in the past there was Father Brown, Doctor Thorndyke. Even Holmes began in stories.

The occult and the horrific certainly flourish, even in miniature. So does science fiction. And all of these provide seams for excavation.

The writer cannot be a slave to fashion, but as I said at the very beginning the short story is a child of its market. The market is where we shall find our audience, and among them we can discover our voice.

2. For the library shelf

Selling short stories is not easy, especially to hardcover publishers. As long as twenty years ago a number of major houses were refusing to consider them. That being said, fashions change. In the intervening period several authors have been very successful when breaking into print with collections of stories, Ian McEwan conspicuous among them; so publishers' editors have begun to think again. They may be hoping to snare a later novel or piece of non-fiction; but strong and recognizable talent is not likely to be turned away.

The author will need to be ruthlessly self-critical. That has already been evident. A dozen stories, of which six are brilliant and six are make-weights, will no longer make a book. It will be helpful if the stories seem all of a piece, have a style, a mood, a way of dealing with life which is common to them all; or if they are pithily counterpointed and juxtaposed. It is a book that is on offer, not a rag bag of bits and pieces. A collection of stories that have the same central character, or explore relationships between the same group of characters, may well have an edge. I think of Brian Glanville's football collections (*Goalkeepers are Crazy* is an excellent title) and of Herriot's episodic vet. An editor could just come to feel that such a proposition might have something to offer to novel readers as well as the people who buy stories — a tiny and select band.

There are always specialists, and publishers who can be persuaded to cater for them. In many cases there are specialist publishers. Fishermen will buy fishing stories, and yachtsmen and yachtswomen will devour things that deal with boats. It is worth remembering the specialist when attempting to place a story with a magazine. There are periodical publications unique to everything from archery to xylophones, indeed to zoos: but fiction is different from jobbing journalism, however honourable the latter. A writer generally needs to have a deep feeling for something before he can work it into creative literature. Jewish stories tend to be written by Jews. If an author thinks something is exotic he will make a mess of it. It is the reader who must feel it is exotic.

At the least, try to find an edge. Ian McEwan was successful because of his surprising treatment of sex. The subject itself is, as they say, an old one. I had thirty stories once, and none of them placed in magazines. It struck me suddenly that fifteen of them concerned unpleasant people speaking (or squeaking and grunting) in the first person. The first publisher to see the new format took it. I am now writing a collection of witches, and I have not the least doubt it will sell.

Incidentally, there is a substantial and genuine market for horror and occult collections, and a possible one for science fiction and fantasy. Again, these are for experts and for *experts in the genre*. The latter, in particular, require persistent imagining. Their worlds have coherencies that cannot be improvized as the story unfolds.

To have published some of your stories in magazines will not effect a hardcover house one way or the other. If you have become famous in the process it will, of course, be a substantial asset. (In general fame is an excellent attribute for an author. If your books are in the public eye then you do not need to be. If you are in the public eye, your books certainly will be too.) If you can interest a paperback publisher this is quite another matter: a swift prop and cop is a near certainty, but you will need to know the field and play it.

If you are a British author, it will undoubtedly help to have an American publisher. English publication is likely to follow. The reverse process does not apply to American authors. American publishers are supremely blind to English fashion, unless it is causing an enormous bow-wave.

Ideally, to make all or any of this happen, you need an agent. Agents are in general reluctant to take on people who only have first collections of stories to offer, still less a small folio of individual stories. Genius *can* persuade, however; and although some agents say there is no profit in short stories, others do very nicely for their authors indeed.

Unless you take the eye of a principal in the firm you are

likely to find that stories are handled by someone very junior. I know my own fortunes were changing, but my stories were handled down the years by several people in an agency, with almost total lack of success. A new girl arrived and sold seven of them as one-offs in a day, including two to *Esquire* in the States for an astronomical sum. Selling is as chancy and as magical as that. Let me also keep the record straight by adding that the *Esquire* fiction editor was given his marching orders the following month and all of his contracts were repudiated.

3. *Magazines*

This is a waning, if not a collapsing, market; but as with stars there is an occasional flare of brightness. (Women's magazines are the exception and I will deal with them in the next chapter.) The attraction is that some magazines, particularly in the States, pay well.

The golden rule is to study the magazines you intend to sell to. It is no good offering a 'toughy' to a periodical which publishes experimental fiction, literary reviews and poetry. Hotpants writing and explicit sex belong in the ones that offer explicit pictures. There are about two dozen of these: it is worth examining them to establish just how explicit 'explicit' is. Sometimes editorial policies change. I used to sell sober, stolid and fully clad stories to *Mayfair* and the old *King* when it was thought that a little ballast would not come amiss.

A complete list of United Kingdom, African, Australian, Canadian, Indian, Irish, New Zealand and South African periodicals can be found in *Writers' and Artists' Yearbook*. There is also an inventory of the major publishing houses.

This is an invaluable publication and cheap. To buy American information costs money. There are two major sources: *The Writer's Handbook*, published by The Writer Inc., 8 Arlington Street, Boston, Mass., USA 02116 (currently $25.00) and *Writer's Market*, published by The Writer's Digest of Cincinnati, 9933 Alliance Road, Cincinnati, Ohio,

USA 45242. Copies can generally be obtained, together with up-to-date quotations, from Freelance Press Services, 5-9 Bexley Square, Salford, Manchester M3 6DB, telephone 061 832 5079; and from Poplar Press Ltd., 13 Burlington Lodge Studios, Rigault Road, London SW6 4JJ, telephone 01 731 5938.

Whatever market you are writing for, the story should be typed double-spaced one side only on A4 paper. The choice used to be between quarto and foolscap, and it is possible that the fashions in stationery will change once more; but A4 is an agreeable page, less daunting than foolscap, not so mingy as quarto. It also works well with processors and electronic typewriters. (The serious writer is likely to retain some foolscap about the desk, because is it used for radio-plays, and for radio and television *as broadcast* or final scripts. Stories for broadcasting should nonetheless be *submitted* on A4.)

4. *The broadcast story*

One way and another several stories go out on the British airwaves each day, from London, Regional and Local BBC, and from some independent radio. There are also several dozen viable pirate stations which sometimes take material but rarely pay. I am not allowed to advertize these. You can find the ones in your own region by twiddling the knobs on your set. Some of them have astonishingly high audience figures — scarcely ratings — and if fame is the only spur it may well suit you to make use of them.

These and the independents have flexible, or at least variable, length requirements. The BBC works to the quarter of an hour broadcast, minus its top and tail: that is the title, introduction, possible one sentence blurb (theirs to contrive, not yours) and the name of the reader. God ordained that radio burns 10,000 words an hour, so if we do the necessary equation we shall find that the length is 2,250-2,300 words.

The word length should be written clearly and honestly on the front of the script, somewhere below the title and your name. So should your address and telephone number. If the story is too long, it pretty certainly won't be taken. If you tell a lie and it is, then it is pressurizing to have to cut it in the studio, and deeply traumatic to watch someone else cut it for you.

The only radio requirement is that the story be a good one. The chatty, colloquial or dialectical is not necessary — indeed not currently in fashion, though it may return. The theory is that a competent actor or actress should be able to make the written word agreeable to the ear and keep literature in shape in the listener's head.

There needs to be a plot, or a central sequence of events, but otherwise what am I telling you? A linear is likely to be the most satisfactory form, a duplex more difficult but by no means impossible. Angel cake is highly acceptable, indeed in its element. The Bloody Great Wheel and the Balloon cannot fail. Do not, however, go on trying to tempt the producer with a single recipe. He wants to give his audience a varied diet, and that certainly includes a varied diet of you. If he thinks you have come up with a formula he would like to exploit he will say so.

Writers' and Artists' Yearbook or the BBC itself will tell you exactly where to send your stories. Ultimately you will learn when to make individual approaches. An agent will already know. The system is fair. There is no point in trying to circumvent it until asked to do so.

The covering letter is merely a courtesy. Sales talk never sells. The story has got to sell itself.

Chapter Nine

Women's Magazines

1. 'That is not it, not it all. . . .'

In the late nineteen sixties I was examining a student's creative writing file. It consisted of a fragment of autobiography and five short stories. She was submitting them as part of an element in her teaching degree. I thought the autobiography was good and the stories rather better. The moderator was a university professor of English whose scholarship was unfashionably encyclopedic, and who was particularly knowledgeable about Grub Street in the Age of Johnson. 'This is all women's magazine stuff,' he said. 'That's why I suggest Alpha,' I agreed. 'No,' he insisted. 'That is my definition of pure C.'

I asked him if he had ever tried to write for a woman's magazine, whether he had even read one. After all, his Doctor Johnson would have done both if they had been around in his day, from necessity and consequent conviction. He told me he had not and gazed at me sadly over lunch while I explained how difficult it was. I may even have said how good they all were.

We were both wrong in our way. He for not reading any, I for only looking through the ones that had taken my untargetted stories. Nowadays the constraints of my own residency in Grub Street force me to read altogether too many of them, and I know they vary from marvellous to awful, as does the fiction they publish. Everyone is agreed about that. The argument is about which is which. On one matter, though, I must insist I was absolutely right. They are not easy to write for.

I know two women who write for women's magazines, and all kinds of authors, male and female, who are published by them. The difference is essential to grasp.

Any serious writer of short stories who has an agent or who manages to have a collection accepted for hardcover publication is likely to have stories appear in women's magazines. The rights go on offer, and there are fiction editors who regard it as their business to see their readers become acquainted with what *is* on offer, whatever that may be. For work to be accepted in this way, there is obviously no formula. Editors who are free to pursue the above policy have no need to be parochial.

Nor do the rest of them, but they do work to some very exacting rules. If you want to sell to them, it will certainly pay to discover what these are. If you intend to write *in order* to sell to them, then it is essential. What you write to sell in this way is unlikely to sell anywhere else. If you have rigorous, purist views of fiction, or if you know your own approach to writing is personal and inflexible, it will probably be less painful if you do not try.

Of course you will have to read the magazines you intend to write for. Study them carefully and don't let the professor infect you. Nonetheless, I hope you will take some Johnsonian moral advice in the matter. Never contribute, even for bread and butter, to something you cannot bear to read. You are putting your creativity on the line and you don't want it to flap among tatty laundry.

One more thing, and in a practical sense the only thing: most women's magazines are by definition purpose built — not for women, but for a collective abstraction called readership. This readership is supposed to have, or to need to have, a view of the world. You may read the magazine as closely as my professor would if he could so be prevailed upon and miss the implications of its sense of itself, which can be idiosyncratic to the point of absurdity. You spot its fondness for glittering teeth and firm young breasts and miss its dislike of, or mania for, bras and toothpaste. You have a fellow feeling, a creative fondness even, for its kitchens, bathrooms and bedrooms because they are so recognizably and stylishly full of *things*, but overlook its repugnance for all, or certain, brand names. You detect its timid view of sex, sense it prefers desire to fulfilment — the often quoted (and many times written) 'the peace she felt welling through her as she turned and listened to Mark's deep and regular breathing' — or note that it is prepared to be more explicit than you ever felt possible, only to boob (you see the problem of constraint when all things are constrained!) by having Cheryl link a platonic little finger with Martin, because you do not know that girls are not allowed to acknowledge their brothers-in-law, not even in friendship. Nor, and how could you know this, that you must not have a Martin, a Cheryl, nor even a Mark, because it steers an exact course on names.

'And how could you know this?' The magazine in question will tell you. Whether it is for stories, serials or features, nearly all of them have an information sheet, many of them a policy statement, sometimes a brochure offering all things in one. You get it by writing to the fiction editor by name (sometimes simply called *fiction* or *stories*, or story editor; even, more grandly, literary editor) or, if the role is not designated but you have observed the magazine to publish stories, to the editor by title. All magazines print their editorial address at the front or right at the back of each issue; most list and name all of their editorial and production staff on the lead or first copy page.

If there is no such guide, phone and ask. But make a list of questions first, from the general 'Do you have a policy?' right down to points of detail. As a general rule, be reluctant with the phone. The person you will be phoning will be operating a production schedule, often a hectic one. So a thirty second phone call will be quite enough. Longer may make her resolve never to forget you.

2. *What is different is plain from the wrapping*

I said that a letter with a broadcast story is no more than a courtesy, by which I meant it should not discuss the story. Here you need a little more, though not necessarily in the letter.

Your name, and somewhere your address, should appear on the title page. So should the number of words. This is standard practice. Since you are writing to a formula, you are likely to be bought to formula. You cannot put this sort of point to an editor, even if she or he (the likely order here) is your best friend. They will always answer, 'I only accept what is good. I only publish what I like.' This is manifestly untrue, since they all print things that absolutely nobody could like, including, unless I am an egg, the readership.

So your title page needs to carry a brief summary, a little blurb, a something.

It should not be a piece of self-commendation —

'Another sensation from the pen of Lesbia Troon!'

Nor even:

'From the squalid swamps of lust a gentler beast arises.'

The one tells what should already be known or is otherwise a lie, the other summarizes everything else in the in-tray.

There is, alas, always scope for a belly-laugh, but:

'Molly loves Marcus, but he prefers his bike'

is not unhelpful; nor is

'Marcus wants to marry, but Molly is a competition dancer'

and it is useful to know that 'Black Tie' explores intrigues among the formation team, and is not about Dracula or romance in the funeral parlour. Editors have their resistance to words that at best are purpose-spun, so it can really help to realize that on the week the magazine is gearing itself to look at incest or child-abuse or drugs here is a knowledgeable piece of fiction on the same subject.

Indeed, if you feel that your story has a topical interest of any kind, then say so, in a sentence, in your covering letter. If you think the story has a purely transient topicality, now while the solo yachtswoman is still beating shorewards, then this is the only time you should consider a simultaneous submission to more than one journal. Book publishers have time to forget, and will forgive an author almost anything, except lack of success. But it is daft to offend a magazine you want to deal with again next week or next month.

(You can't, of course, *sell* to more than one journal, only *offer*. If you are into the business of 'Dutch Auctions' you certainly need an agent.)

3. *And when you undo the string?*

I have before me one of the successful ventures across the publication minefield. Good money was paid, but the Muse blew her legs off.

She lugged her overstuffed valise down from the ticket-littered footplate of the trolley-bus and stepped across a beggar-strewn sidewalk — hardly a pavement — towards the hotel portico.

She supposed portico was the word. There were pillars, plaster mouldings, potted plants and windows in ornate glass and two revolving doors.

Esmeralda hesitated for the first time in her life. In part it was because she was tired, but what really stopped her dead in her tracks was one of those weird hallucinations only tiredness can induce. The revolving doors framed panels so dusty she did not realize they were glass. They were grey and opaque, and in the dawn sunlit they acted like mirrors — spinning, revolving, disorientating mirrors in which she glimpsed her own person, her jaded anxious face, her taut young body with the firm breasts and torn blouse, somehow etched grey and spidery as any ghost in the thrown-off lid of its coffin.

Her coffin! She had not forgotten that night in Calcutta, the ugly moments in the hearse-shed, and especially not her encounter with Patel and the water-seller in the Christian cemetery. Nor, at this moment, could her youthful imaginings relinquish . . .

and so on. But someone prints it and gives the rest of us a glimpse of where we have been going wrong all these years.

Other magazines share this fondness for the Bloody Great Wheel. Here is a story that gets on with the action but still tries to do too much:

Susan stood awkwardly, her suitcase straining her arm, her body leaning sideways to cope with its weight. She knew she could still turn away — but she wouldn't. Her fate for the rest of the summer was still in her hands, and yet she had already taken the plunge. She had made the decision back home in Ealing when she had gone to the job centre and said she had enough experience to help in a country kitchen specializing in 'plain meals for guests who prefer English cooking'! That was what the yellow card had said, Susan's cooking *was* plain, and she needed the money.

What the yellow card hadn't explained was that the 'country kitchen' was in a castle in the middle of a lake, and that the old wooden bridge that led to it was much too frail to take her taxi.

So Susan had to gather up her case and walk across the duck-boards above the lily pads and stagger towards the huge front door.

There wasn't a knocker, and she couldn't see a bell. There was a length of chain hanging from the ivy overhead.

Susan tugged at it without success, so she began to swing it to and fro against the door.

The noise . . .

It is interesting to see how the magazine draws attention to this story, which is called *Cooking up Love*. In the contents column, called FIRST LOOK, we read: 'Take a pretty girl, add some sun — and hope that too many cooks don't spoil the romance'. On the title page, in bold type: 'Seated at the table was just about the best-looking young man that Susan had ever seen in her life'; then, lower down the page, in case interest flags or is never kindled, we read, also in bold: 'Swathed in bandages and unable to cook, he supervised her every move, issuing precise instructions to a scared but blissful Susan'. Magazines write their own blurbs and select the extracts; but if this were your story, it could well pay you to type the second extract at the head of your title, somewhere. Such a ploy is informative without suggesting swollen-headedness on the part of the author. Most magazines print their stories with a flier, and will be used to buying them that way. Above another story, in a magazine whose attitude is both modern and feminist, a very old question poses itself: 'Could they share a career and still find happiness?' and again, even more specifically, 'What would her job do to her love-life?'

In a small fan of current up-market magazines, splayed around the typewriter, I can read stories by William Trevor, Michele Roberts, Francis King, Angela Carter and John McGahern. Some of these are from collections, and it is in this area that editors seem prepared to take risks. *Cosmopolitan*, a magazine I enjoy, is perhaps the most eclectic. Last month it printed two stories, each of which — one for exoticism, one for experimentation — seem surprising choices. This one, for instance, breaks every common sense rule of sale:

> His name means saviour. He rolls into your arms like Ozzie and Harriet, the whole Nelson genealogy. He is living rooms and turkey and mantels and Vicks, a nip at the collarbone and you do a slow syrup sink into those arms like a hearth, into those living rooms, well hello Mary Lou. Say you work in an office but you have bigger plans. He wants to go with you. He wants to be what it is

that you want to be. Say you are an aspiring architect. Playwright. Painter. He shows you his sketches. They are awful. What do you think?

Put on some jazz. Take off your clothes. Carefully. It is a craft. He will lie on the floor naked, watching. . . .

Yes, it is a craft, but this is for your consolation. Here is something that seems to exemplify everything we have been looking for throughout this book. It is simple, fresh, and comes immediately to the point:

My parents adopted Alice before they figured out my mother was already pregnant with me. And people when they hear we're sisters will say, 'Oh yes, you look just alike. Around the eyes.' Alice and I don't look anything alike . . . Alice has always stood out, her smile brilliant like lightning.

So now we know. This is by Mary Morris and is in *Woman's Journal*. It is from her collection *The Bus of Dreams*. It is obviously about jealousy and conflict. The conflict climaxes in physical confrontation. There is reconciliation. It is a good old-fashioned linear.

Chapter Ten

Keeping On

1. *The Garner*

When your first story is finished, make a fuss of it. Get a manila folder, write its title on the cover and clip two slips of paper inside — one to note alternative titles and the page numbers of important revisions, the other to list all the places you send it (and under what title it is submitted to each outlet).

Put your rough copy, your working typescript and any carbons or notes in the folder; then take your best typescript to be photographed. Then file your best typescript as well: you may need to make extra copies, and photocopies sometimes fade, so it is worth going back to a sharp original text.

Each story is a production run. That is why it needs its own warehouse. You hope to sell it to be broadcast, published in a magazine, collected into a book and perhaps anthologized. You have transatlantic and world aspirations as well. That's *six* copies even if all your first shots are successful; and hardcover publishers who say 'yes' have a habit of asking for other copies, for promotions, the jacket artist, and for the 'rights' department to show paperback publishing houses. Your house editor can take a photograph, or have one taken or wait for a proof; and some authors — self-regarding so-called professionals — think that this is an expense best born by the publisher. What you lose by taking this view is the period of time someone is prepared to devote to advancing your interest, and you lose it now, while that person's enthusiasm is hot. So, if a hardcover publisher accepts you, leave some numbered copies with your editor. Then if somebody phones you they can be told where to find them at once.

As your output progresses, still use a separate folder for each new story. When it is printed, file the offprints, cuttings or 'as broadcast' script away with it as well.

This is very good for your ego and sense of order. More importantly, it is a reminder that the story-writer — *you* — thinks primarily in single stories. I once wasted a lot of time scolding two early stories for not fitting an intended collection. I shuffled them in and out of the pile of typescripts and up and down the order of contents. It was a long time before I realized they were not only different from my other work but very much better. If I had kept them apart, and afforded them a proper respect, I should have known this from the beginning.

I suggest filing rough notes and first drafts because of their usefulness to you during a fallow period. One mark of maturity as a writer is the cutting of good work as well as bad from a script. 'What an excellent paragraph,' you think, 'what a pithy exchange of dialogue,' followed so often by, 'what a pity I am so overweighed by genius I have gone on too long!'

The passage may not belong here, but it can sometimes enjoy a fruitful life as a transplant. More, the sentence that was rejected as a distracting digression is often the seed of a fresh idea.

A manila folder is a small enough outlay. The first time you *sell* a story you should make a real commitment to space and privacy. Domestic living is not easy for the writer; but success should entitle you at least to your own desk or table, or your own bureau and corner shelf.

The ideal is to have a room. If gardening can skulk in its little shed, so can writing. Children, surely, should not have the first claim to space, nor their homework make the only demands on silence.

2. 'Writer's Block'

All writers have bad days, days on which we simply cannot get the words to flow. Some of us have indifferent weeks, slack months and unproductive years as well. If we write full time we sense the bills forming up and hear them begin to march towards us.

A block is often worse for the amateur. The bills can take care of themselves, or not, much as they always did. Time is the expensive commodity. We can give ourself an hour each evening, say, and an early Sunday morning, all without domestic complaint. But if we cannot fill that space, others will. Fine if we can sit and sulk and pretend. What happens if we need to kick the furniture and storm out of doors?

There is only one answer, the maddening one: don't. As the Duke of Wellington said of insomnia, 'No good will come of it, so I positively don't advise it!' The first block — ask any author — is the one that stops us reaching the desk. So take a jug of tea, coffee or scotch and sit there and drink it.

Have an alternative task ready at the desk. For example, I loathe typing. I would rather starve and pay a typist than do my own typing; but I always keep a small piece of work by my typewriter and use it to punish myself if the pen refuses to flow. If you make a serious commitment to authorship, you will shortly be busy with more concerns than one. Even if you have an orderly mind whose Muse makes uncomplicated demands, you will soon find yourself writing one piece of work, revising another and making notes for a third. I know no-one who cannot revise or make notes and research. It is the writing that stops us.

So does that word 'work'. I had published seven books amid much bewilderment but total joy before I took on a screenplay and decided to call writing 'work'. It has given me intermittent pain ever since.

The part-timer should think positively about his fixed hours. They are times of retreat, solitude, recreation, not exile. If the pen won't flow, the desk is still a good place to read and make notes. Read your own work at such times. Learn to be your own favourite author. If you don't like what you write, resolve to think better of it. Take a piece of rough paper and give yourself a mark for every good effect you achieve in the story you are reading. If you enjoy a joke, a brisk exchange, a bold shift of paragraph, award yourself a star. Your critical abilities will not be diminished thereby. The trouble with us all is that we sit over our work until we cannot see it. We frustrate ourselves with our inadequacies, instead of celebrating our energies. That is where the block comes.

Never ask the family. The family will always purse its lips, damn with faint praise or be gushingly loyal and fulsome. There is a degree of self-exposure in all art, and frankly everything you do is an embarrassment to your nearest and dearest.

The full-timer knows all this. The professional — and some of you will become professionals — has a different problem. It is, simply expressed, how to stop the working day becoming sour. We know we must sit at the desk. We know we must shift copy. How can we keep it fresh?

The answer here is to find time away, to study *how* we work and *when* we work, and to brood less on what we work at. The best way was indicated by Trollope and practised by Tolstoy, and it is there for all resolute minds. It is to rise early and do a day's work by lunchtime. The aim is to create hours *away* from work. The work has to be done, but it does more damage to the mind than carpentry or cobbling, so we need to rest the pineal eye.

Some of us are resolute but not orderly. Or we have (as Trollope's contemporary critics pretended to have) more respect for inspiration. Then we must divide the day or the week into segments and make sure we fill enough of them with activity.

I am one of these. I believe in inspiration, in waiting for the words to flow rather than be forced, because I know that *for me* they flow faster and read more easily. So when the words run, I stop whatever else I am doing and trap them.

This method also has its penalties and requires an equal measure of self-compassion. The words sometimes come for

Useful Reading

1. Historic Perspective

Dent's Everyman has collected de Maupassant, and Chekhov is cheaply served in a series of Penguin editions. The beginnings of the macabre and of detective fiction can be found in the Collected Writings of Edgar Allan Poe, published by Doubleday. Early demotic humour is well represented by Artemus Ward (C. F. Browne) *Artemus Ward His Book*, and the best edition is the 1888 Routledge, though this is a matter for second-hand bookshops or a lucky library. O. Henry can be found in most libraries in a variety of collections and selections. Saki needs to be read entire, but he is in and out of print. The old World Books edition is an excellent one — though again it is something to pounce on in a jumble-sale — but until that lucky moment we can be well content with Tom Sharpe's *The Best of Saki* published by Picador.

I said in Chapter One that the short story cannot easily be separated from its means of publication. *Argosy*, long defunct, used to be the best market-place in the world for short stories. It looks more like a paperback book than a magazine, and can often be seen mixed in with the paperbacks in junk-shops. Any number is worth snapping up and fumigating, at least while the price is low. There are stories there by Kersch, Ray Bradbury and even H. E. Bates that have not been collected.

2. Ongoing Fare

Since the short story is so recent a phenomenon, it is hard to separate its yesterdays. From Penguin we can obtain most Hemingway, *The Collected Short Stories* of Katherine Mansfield, the overrated but intermittently brilliant *The Stories of John Cheever*, some of John Updike (the rest from Deutsch), G. K. Chesterton's *The Penguin Complete Father Brown*, and the *Selected Stories* of Nadine Gordimer.

Camus' *Exile and the Kingdom* is not now in print with Penguin, but failing a chance encounter with an old copy it can be found at the back of *The Collected Fiction of Albert Camus*, published by Hamish Hamilton. Deutsch publish Wolf Mankowitz' *The Mendelman Fire*, and Methuen Milovan Djilas' *The Leper*. Secker and Warburg have published a number of collections by Moravia — a very cold fish — but the 41 pieces in *The Fetish* are worth the chilly reading. James Purdy's *Children is All* and *Colour of Darkness* are also published by Secker.

Of the writers I suggest in the main text, David Pownall (Faber) and Alex Hamilton (Hutchinson) are not in current print, but are to be demanded in libraries.

431530